SPIRITUAL DETOX

Cleansing the Soul and Rewriting Your DNA for Divine Alignment

PASTOR DR. CLAUDINE BENJAMIN

For more information or to book an event, contact:
inspiredtowinsouls@gmail.com

Published by:

Editor: Cleveland O. McLeish (Author C. Orville McLeish)

ISBN: 978-1-965635-75-9 (paperback)

Dedication

This book is dedicated first and foremost to my Lord and Savior, Jesus Christ—the ultimate Healer, Redeemer, and Restorer of the soul. Without His grace, mercy, and cleansing power, there would be no hope of renewal or true freedom.

To every weary soul searching for peace, to every believer longing for a fresh start, and to every broken vessel desiring wholeness— this work is for you. May these words remind you that God still heals, God still restores, and God still renews.

I also dedicate this book to my family, whose prayers, encouragement, and love have been a steady anchor through every season of my journey. Your faith has strengthened mine, and your unwavering support has helped me to walk boldly in obedience to the call of God.

And to the countless men and women of God who labor faithfully in prayer, fasting, and consecration—may this book strengthen your hands and ignite a new passion to pursue holiness and wholeness in every area of life.

Acknowledgment

I humbly acknowledge the hand of Almighty God in the writing of this book. It is only by His Spirit that the message of Spiritual Detox has been birthed, shaped, and carried to completion. All glory belongs to Him.

My deepest gratitude goes to my family, who have stood beside me with patience, love, and prayer. Thank you for believing in the vision God has placed in me and for allowing me the space and time to pour my heart into this work.

I also want to thank my church family and spiritual mentors who have encouraged me, corrected me, and interceded for me along the way. Your words and your witness have been a constant reminder that true transformation begins when we fully yield to God.

To every friend, intercessor, and supporter who has prayed, offered words of encouragement, or shared testimonies that inspired these pages—this book carries pieces of your faith and resilience.

Finally, to every reader who will take this journey of detox with me—thank you. You are the reason this book was written. My prayer is that as you read, you will experience the cleansing power of God, the renewing of your mind, and the restoration of your spirit, body, and soul.

About the Author

Pastor Claudine Benjamin is a devoted servant of God, passionate about leading souls into deeper relationship with Christ and guiding believers toward spiritual maturity. With a heart for evangelism, discipleship, and restoration, she has spent her life teaching, preaching, and writing to help others experience the transforming power of God's Word.

As a pastor, intercessor, and mentor, Pastor Claudine has witnessed firsthand the struggles many face when burdened by sin, shame, and spiritual toxins. Out of this burden came the message of Spiritual Detox, a guide to cleansing the soul, renewing the mind, and restoring the body through the truth of scripture and practical life applications.

Her writings are marked by urgency, compassion, and a deep reliance on the power of the Holy Spirit. She believes in speaking truth with love, equipping the church to walk in holiness, and calling every believer to embrace their God-given purpose.

Beyond the pulpit, Pastor Claudine is also a voice of encouragement to families, leaders, and those who have been wounded by life's storms. She writes not only from biblical knowledge but also from personal experiences of resilience, faith, and overcoming.

Her mission is clear: to see souls saved, lives transformed, and the church empowered to live victoriously in Christ.

When she is not writing or ministering, Pastor Claudine enjoys moments of quiet reflection, studying God's Word, and inspiring others through teaching and mentorship.

Spiritual Detox is one of her many contributions to the body of Christ, continuing her legacy of faith, hope, and a relentless pursuit of God's glory.

Table of Contents

Dedication iii

Acknowledgment v

About the Author vii

Introduction 11

Part I

Understanding Detox

Chapter 1: What Is Detox? – Natural and Spiritual Perspective 15

Chapter 2: Why We Need a Detox – Removing Toxins from Body, Mind, and Spirit 21

Chapter 3: The Connection Between the Natural and the Spiritual 27

Chapter 4: Signs You Need a Detox – Spiritually, Mentally, and Physically 33

Part II

Spiritual Detox

Chapter 5: Detoxing the Soul – Releasing Sin, Guilt, and Shame 41

Chapter 6: Detoxing the Mind – Renewing Your Thoughts with the Word of God 47

Chapter 7: Detoxing the Heart – Forgiveness, Healing, and Letting Go of Offense 53

Chapter 8: Detoxing the Spirit – Prayer, Fasting, and Worship as Cleansing Tools 59

Chapter 9: Breaking Strongholds and Spiritual Addictions 65

Chapter 10: Maintaining a Clean Spirit – Daily Habits for Purity and Growth 71

Part III

Natural Detox

Chapter 11: The Body as God's Temple – Why Physical Health Matters .. 79

Chapter 12: Nutrition for Cleansing – Foods That Heal and Restore 85

Chapter 13: Fasting and Its Benefits – Natural and Spiritual Renewal 91

Chapter 14: Prayer and Meditation – Detoxing the Mind and Spirit 97

Chapter 15: Worship as a Form of Detox – Cleansing Through Praise 103

Part IV

Living a Detoxed Life

Chapter 16: The Power of Forgiveness – Detoxing the Heart from Bitterness
.... 111

Chapter 17: The Role of Fasting – Detoxing Body and Spirit Together... 117

Chapter 18: Guarding the Gates – Detoxing What You See, Hear, and Speak
.... 123

Chapter 19: Rest as a Detox – Releasing Stress and Finding God's Peace
.... 129

Chapter 20: Forgiveness as Detox – Letting Go of Emotional Poisons.... 135

Chapter 21: The Word as Detox – Renewing the Mind Daily 141

Chapter 22: Worship as Detox – Clearing the Atmosphere of the Soul ... 147

Chapter 23: Prayer as Detox – Flushing Out the Soul's Burdens 153

Chapter 24: Fasting as Detox – Cleansing Both Body and Spirit 157

Chapter 25: Guarding the Gateways – Protecting the Mind, Heart, and Spirit
.... 163

Chapter 26: A Lifestyle of Purity and Holiness 169

Conclusion: The Final Charge: A Life Detoxed and Fully Alive 175

Introduction

We live in a world saturated with noise, distractions, and toxic influences that often leave our souls heavy, weary, and burdened. Just as the body requires a cleansing process to rid itself of harmful toxins, the spirit also needs intentional renewal to remain healthy, vibrant, and connected to God. Spiritual detox is not a luxury—it is a necessity for every believer who desires to walk in freedom, clarity, and power.

The truth is, many of us carry the weight of past hurts, unconfessed sins, unhealthy habits, and lingering doubts that quietly poison our relationship with God. These spiritual toxins may not always be visible. Still, their effects are real—manifesting in broken fellowship with God, lack of peace, diminished faith, and an inability to hear His voice clearly. Just as neglecting the body can lead to sickness, neglecting the spirit can hinder our growth, effectiveness, and ultimate destiny in Christ.

This book is an invitation to pause, reflect, and allow the Holy Spirit to search every corner of your heart. It is a call to release what no longer serves your walk with God and embrace the fresh, cleansing flow of His presence. Through scripture, reflection, and practical application, Spiritual Detox will guide you on a journey of purification, renewal, and restoration.

As you read these pages, you will discover that spiritual detox is not about rules or rituals—it is about surrender. It is about returning to the One who promised, **"Behold, I make all things new"**

(Revelation 21:5). It is about letting God strip away the old and replace it with His truth, His peace, and His power.

My prayer is that this journey will not only cleanse your heart but also awaken a deeper hunger for God's presence. May you come to experience the freedom that comes when the weights are lifted, the chains are broken, and the soul is refreshed by the living water of Christ.

Let us begin this journey together—emptying ourselves of the things that defile, and opening ourselves fully to the One who purifies, sanctifies, and renews.

Part I

Understanding Detox

Chapter 1

What Is Detox? – Natural and Spiritual Perspective

In today's world, the word *detox* often calls to mind juicing, herbal teas, cleanses, or fasting from unhealthy foods. But detox is far more than a health trend; it is a process of removing harmful substances—whether in the body, the mind, or the spirit—so that life can flourish in its purest form. Just as our physical bodies must be cleansed of toxins to function properly, so must our souls and spirits be renewed from the contamination of sin, negative thinking, and worldly influences.

God designed the human being as a three-part creation—spirit, soul, and body (**see 1 Thessalonians 5:23**). Each part affects the others. A neglected body can weigh down the spirit; a troubled mind can poison the heart; and an unclean spirit can manifest in physical and emotional struggles. Therefore, detox is not optional—it is essential for living the abundant life Jesus promised (**see John 10:10**).

The Natural Concept of Detox

In the physical sense, detox refers to the body's natural process of eliminating waste and harmful substances. The liver, kidneys, lungs, skin, and digestive system all serve as God's built-in cleansing system. However, when we overload our bodies with processed foods, toxins from the environment, stress, and lack of rest, these systems struggle. That's when we feel fatigued, sluggish, or unwell.

Natural detox practices such as drinking water, eating whole foods, exercising, and resting help restore the body's God-given rhythm. It is not about starvation or quick fixes, but about aligning with the Creator's design. In fact, biblical figures often practiced what we would now call detox. Daniel chose vegetables and water instead of the king's rich food (**see Daniel 1:12**), and his health flourished. God always honors purity—whether physical or spiritual.

The Spiritual Concept of Detox

If the body needs detoxification, how much more does the spirit? Sin, bitterness, unforgiveness, fear, pride, and unhealthy attachments all function like toxins in the soul. They weigh us down, contaminate our thinking, and block the flow of God's Spirit. Isaiah 59:2 reminds us that **"your iniquities have separated you from your God; your sins have hid his face from you." (KJV).** A spiritual detox is necessary to reconnect with God, to remove the things that hinder intimacy, and to restore clarity of vision.

Spiritual detox happens when we:

- Confess and repent of sin (**see 1 John 1:9**).
- Release unforgiveness and bitterness (**see Ephesians 4:31–32**).
- Saturate our minds with God's Word (**see Romans 12:2**).
- Fast and pray to quiet the flesh and strengthen the spirit (**see Matthew 6:16–18**).

- Worship and praise as cleansing streams that wash away heaviness (**see Isaiah 61:3**).

Just as a clogged artery prevents life-giving blood from flowing, so a soul clogged with spiritual toxins blocks the life of the Spirit. Detox is the process of opening the channel again so that God's presence can flow unhindered.

The Connection Between Natural and Spiritual Detox

Natural detox is not separate from spiritual detox—it often works hand in hand. When you fast from certain foods, you discover how dependent you are on physical cravings, and God uses that moment to teach you dependence on Him. When you drink more water, you're reminded of Jesus as the Living Water (**see John 4:14**). When you let go of toxic environments, it mirrors the spiritual principle of leaving sin and embracing holiness.

Detox is a picture of consecration. In both the natural and the spiritual, it is about cleansing, purifying, and returning to God's original intent.

Signs You Need a Detox

You know your body needs a detox when you feel tired, heavy, or inflamed. Likewise, your spirit needs a detox when:

- You feel distant from God despite attending church.
- Prayer feels dry, forced, or non-existent.
- Old sins or habits creep back in.
- Your heart is weighed down with bitterness, anger, or fear.
- You are constantly distracted, restless, or without peace.

These signs are not to condemn you, but to awaken you. Just as physical pain signals the body that something is wrong, so spiritual heaviness alerts the believer that a cleansing is needed.

The Goal of Detox

Detox is not about deprivation—it is about restoration. The goal is clarity, purity, and alignment with God's will. When the body is cleansed, energy returns. When the spirit is cleansed, joy is restored. When the mind is renewed, peace rules. The end result of detox is freedom: freedom from what once bound you and freedom to live fully in God's purpose.

Psalm 51:10 becomes our prayer: **"Create in me a clean heart, O God; and renew a right spirit within me." (KJV).**

Reflection Questions

1. In what ways have you experienced toxins—physically, mentally, or spiritually—in your life?

2. What are some habits or influences that may be weighing you down?

3. How do you see the connection between natural detox and spiritual renewal?

Prayer

Heavenly Father, I come before You acknowledging that I need Your cleansing power in every area of my life. Wash me from sin, purify my heart, and renew my mind. Help me to release every toxin—whether from my body, my soul, or my spirit—that blocks me from living fully in You. May I walk in the freshness of Your Spirit and the strength of Your Word. In Jesus' name. Amen.

Declaration

I declare that I am a temple of the Holy Spirit. I release every weight, sin, and toxin that does not belong in my life. I embrace the cleansing power of God's Spirit, and I walk in freedom, purity, and restoration.

Chapter 2

Why We Need a Detox – Removing Toxins from Body, Mind, and Spirit

When something in your body is out of order, you notice it. Fatigue, headaches, digestive problems, or brain fog all serve as warning signals that your system is overloaded. In the same way, when your spirit and soul are burdened by sin, worry, or toxic influences, you may feel disconnected from God, emotionally drained, or spiritually powerless. Just as the body cannot thrive when weighed down with impurities, neither can the spirit soar when it is clouded with spiritual toxins.

The need for detox is not a suggestion—it is a necessity. From the beginning, God's desire has been that His people walk in purity and freedom.

"Ye shall be holy: for I the Lord your God am holy." (Leviticus 19:2 - KJV).

Yet the world around us constantly introduces pollutants—whether through food, thoughts, media, relationships, or environments. Without intentional cleansing, both the natural and spiritual parts of us become compromised.

The Reality of Toxins in the Body

Our bodies are God's temple (**see 1 Corinthians 6:19–20**). Yet in our fast-paced, convenience-driven world, we often feed it foods loaded with preservatives, sugar, and chemicals. Add stress, lack of exercise, and environmental pollution, and suddenly the body struggles to carry out its God-designed functions.

Physical toxins can cause:

- Sluggishness and lack of energy.
- Frequent illness or weakened immunity.
- Inflammation and chronic pain.
- Premature aging.

Ignoring these warning signs only makes matters worse. That is why natural detox practices like fasting, hydration, whole foods, and rest are so powerful—they help the body recover the balance God intended.

The Reality of Toxins in the Mind

Equally important are the toxins that cloud our thoughts. The Bible urges us: **"Set your minds on things above, not on earthly things" (Colossians 3:2 - NIV).** Yet our minds are constantly bombarded with negativity, comparison, lust, fear, and endless distractions. Social media, entertainment, and toxic conversations can poison our perspective if left unchecked.

Mental toxins often manifest as:

- Anxiety and fear.
- Constant comparison and low self-worth.

- Negative thought cycles.
- Difficulty focusing or hearing God's voice.

Romans 12:2 reminds us that transformation comes through the renewing of the mind. A mental detox requires replacing lies with truth, saturating our minds with scripture, and choosing to dwell on what is pure and praiseworthy (**see Philippians 4:8**).

The Reality of Toxins in the Spirit

Spiritual toxins are perhaps the most dangerous because they separate us from God. Just as Adam and Eve hid in shame after disobedience (**see Genesis 3:8–10**), unrepented sin still drives us away from God's presence. Bitterness, pride, lust, greed, and idolatry are not just "bad habits"—they are spiritual toxins that pollute the soul.

When the spirit is burdened, it often shows up in life as:

- Prayerlessness or a lack of desire for God.
- Compromise in values and integrity.
- Spiritual dryness and lack of discernment.
- Repeated cycles of sin and defeat.

The good news is that God has already provided the cleansing solution through Christ's blood.

"If we confess our sins, he is faithful and just and will forgive us our sins and purify us from all unrighteousness." (1 John 1:9 - NIV).

A spiritual detox is not about striving to be clean—it is about surrendering to the One who makes us clean.

Why Detox Is Essential for Wholeness

The human being is a three-part creation—spirit, soul, and body. When one part is polluted, the others suffer. A toxic body can lead to depression. A toxic mind can weaken the immune system. A toxic spirit can rob us of peace and strength.

Detox is God's invitation to wholeness:

- Physically, to honor Him with our bodies.
- Mentally, to align our thoughts with His truth.
- Spiritually, to walk in intimacy and purity before Him.

Jesus said in John 15:2, **"Every branch in me that beareth not fruit he taketh away: and every branch that beareth fruit, he purgeth it, that it may bring forth more fruit." (KJV).** Detox is a form of pruning. It cuts away what is harmful so that what is healthy can flourish.

Biblical Examples of Detox

1. **Daniel** – Refused the king's food and drank only water and vegetables, resulting in greater wisdom and health (**see Daniel 1:8–16**).

2. **David** – Prayed for God to cleanse his heart and renew his spirit after falling into sin (**see Psalm 51:10**).

3. **Jesus** – Fasted forty days in the wilderness, overcoming temptation and beginning His ministry in power (**see Matthew 4:1–11**).

Each of these examples shows the necessity of both natural and spiritual cleansing to prepare for a greater purpose.

Reflection Questions

1. Which area of your life—body, mind, or spirit—feels the most weighed down right now?

2. What are some "toxins" (habits, influences, or attitudes) that you may need to release?

3. How might a season of intentional detox position you to hear God more clearly?

Prayer

Lord, I recognize that I have allowed toxins into my life—physically, mentally, and spiritually. I repent of the things that have weighed me down and separated me from You. Cleanse me, purify me, and restore me. Help me to honor You with my body as Your temple, with my mind as a place of truth, and with my spirit as a dwelling for Your presence. In Jesus' name. Amen.

Declaration

I declare that I am free from every toxin that has weighed me down. My body is healthy, my mind is renewed, and my spirit is alive in Christ. I walk in purity, clarity, and wholeness through the cleansing power of God.

Chapter 3

The Connection Between the Natural and the Spiritual

We live in a culture that often separates the physical from the spiritual, as if what we eat, how we think, and how we live have no bearing on our walk with God. Yet scripture makes it clear that the natural and the spiritual are deeply connected. Our physical health can impact our spiritual effectiveness, and our spiritual state can influence our physical well-being. When one area is burdened, the others often follow.

Paul declared in 1 Thessalonians 5:23, **"And the very God of peace sanctify you wholly; and I pray God your whole spirit and soul and body be preserved blameless unto the coming of our Lord Jesus Christ." (KJV).** Notice—God desires wholeness in all three areas, not just one. Detox, whether natural or spiritual, is not about focusing on one part while neglecting the others, but about alignment and balance.

Biblical Foundation for Natural-Spiritual Connection

Throughout scripture, we see that God used physical practices to reveal spiritual truths:

- **Fasting** – While it involved abstaining from food, the deeper purpose was always to humble the soul before God and increase sensitivity to His Spirit (**see Ezra 8:21, Matthew 6:16–18**).

- **Water** – Essential for physical life, but also a symbol of spiritual cleansing and renewal. Jesus called Himself the Living Water (**see John 4:14**).

- **Bread** – A staple for nourishment, but also a symbol of Christ, the Bread of Life (**see John 6:35**).

- **Oil** – Used in natural healing and anointing, but also symbolic of the Holy Spirit's empowerment (**see James 5:14, Acts 10:38**).

God repeatedly uses natural elements as teaching tools for spiritual reality. This means that when we undergo a natural detox, we are invited to reflect on the spiritual parallels—purging what is harmful, restoring purity, and creating space for God's presence.

How the Natural Impacts the Spiritual

A body weighed down with toxins, fatigue, or sickness can affect your spiritual life. It's difficult to pray with focus, worship with passion, or serve with joy when you are physically drained. Elijah, after his victory on Mount Carmel, became so physically and emotionally exhausted that he wished to die. What did God do? He sent an angel to feed him and give him rest (**see 1 Kings 19:4–8**). Elijah's spiritual strength was restored after his physical needs were met.

Likewise, lack of discipline in physical life often bleeds into spiritual life. Overeating, addiction, or neglecting rest can dull spiritual sensitivity. Paul spoke of disciplining his body so that he would not be disqualified from his calling (**see 1 Corinthians 9:27**). The principle is clear: when the natural is out of balance, it can hinder spiritual clarity.

How the Spiritual Impacts the Natural

The opposite is also true—what happens in your spirit can manifest in your body. Proverbs 17:22 says, **"A merry heart doeth good like a medicine: but a broken spirit drieth the bones." (KJV).** Anxiety, fear, unforgiveness, and bitterness are spiritual toxins that can lead to stress-related illnesses, high blood pressure, insomnia, and weakened immunity.

Forgiveness, peace, and joy—fruits of a detoxed spirit—have healing effects on the body. Studies confirm what the Bible has long taught: releasing bitterness lowers stress, practicing gratitude improves physical health, and prayer reduces anxiety. The natural thrives when the spiritual is cleansed.

Jesus as the Perfect Example

Jesus modeled a perfect balance between the natural and the spiritual. He fasted, showing discipline over the physical. He prayed, showing dependence on the Father. He walked, ate simply, and spent time in solitude—all natural practices that supported His spiritual mission. His life was proof that when the natural and spiritual are aligned, the result is a life of power, clarity, and fruitfulness.

Detox as an Act of Worship

When you care for your body by eating clean, drinking water, and resting well, you are not just doing it for yourself—you are worshiping God by honoring His temple (**see Romans 12:1**). When you fast, pray, forgive, and surrender your spirit, you are detoxing spiritually and drawing closer to Him.

A true detox is not about vanity or legalism; it is about consecration. It is an act of saying, "Lord, I give You every part of me—my spirit, my soul, and my body."

Practical Steps to Bridge the Two

1. **Pair physical fasting with prayer** – Don't just abstain from food; fill that time with scripture and worship.

2. **Drink more water and meditate on Living Water** – Let natural hydration remind you of the Spirit's refreshing.

3. **Exercise as stewardship** – Move your body with gratitude, remembering it is God's temple.

4. **Practice mental detox daily** – Limit toxic media while feeding on God's Word.

5. **Rest intentionally** – Sleep not just as recovery, but as obedience, trusting God to sustain you.

Reflection Questions

1. How have you seen your physical health affect your spiritual life—or vice versa?

2. Are there habits in your natural life that may be hindering your spiritual clarity?

3. What small step can you take this week to align the natural and spiritual?

Prayer

Lord, thank You for creating me as spirit, soul, and body. I confess that I have often separated what You designed to be connected. Help me to honor You in my natural body as well as in my spirit. Teach me discipline, balance, and alignment. May my health, my thoughts, and my spirit all glorify You as one unified offering. In Jesus' name. Amen.

Declaration

I declare that my spirit, soul, and body are aligned under the Lordship of Christ. My natural health supports my spiritual life, and my spiritual life strengthens my natural body. I live in balance, wholeness, and freedom by the power of God.

Chapter 4

Signs You Need a Detox – Spiritually, Mentally, and Physically

One of the greatest dangers of both physical and spiritual toxins is that they can build up silently. At first, you may not notice the fatigue, the heaviness, or the distance from God. But over time, the signs become more evident. Just as the body gives off warning symptoms when something is wrong, so the spirit and soul send signals that a cleansing is needed.

Recognizing these signs is not about condemnation; it is about awareness. The sooner you detect the buildup of toxins, the sooner you can take steps toward restoration.

Physical Signs You Need a Detox

The body is remarkably honest—it will let you know when something is wrong. Physical toxins often reveal themselves in the following ways:

1. **Chronic Fatigue** – You feel drained even after rest because your body is overburdened.

2. **Digestive Problems** – Bloating, constipation, or irregularity can point to toxin buildup in the gut.

3. **Skin Breakouts** – Acne, rashes, or dull skin often indicate an internal imbalance.

4. **Frequent Illness** – A weak immune system struggles when toxins are present.

5. **Brain Fog** – Difficulty concentrating or remembering details can be linked to a poor diet and overload.

These are not just health inconveniences—they are signals that the body is crying out for cleansing. Remember, your body is the temple of the Holy Spirit (**see 1 Corinthians 6:19–20**). Caring for it is an act of worship.

Mental Signs You Need a Detox

Our minds are daily bombarded with thoughts, images, and messages. When toxic input outweighs truth, the result is a polluted thought life. Some mental signs include:

1. **Negative Thought Patterns** – Constantly expecting the worst, rehearsing past failures, or criticizing yourself.

2. **Anxiety and Fear** – Persistent worry or panic that robs you of peace.

3. **Overwhelm and Distraction** – Difficulty focusing on prayer, scripture, or tasks.

4. **Comparison and Envy** – Social media scrolling or cultural pressure breeds discontent.

5. **Mental Exhaustion** – Always busy in thought, yet never refreshed.

Romans 8:6 warns us: **"For to be carnally minded is death; but to be spiritually minded is life and peace." (KJV).** A mental detox is necessary when the noise of the world drowns out the still, small voice of God.

Spiritual Signs You Need a Detox

The most critical area to examine is the spirit. Spiritual toxins are subtle but dangerous, and they often reveal themselves in ways such as:

1. **Dryness in Prayer and Worship** – Prayer feels like a chore, and worship seems empty.

2. **Compromise with Sin** – What once convicted you no longer bothers you.

3. **Loss of Passion for God's Word** – The Bible sits unopened, and hunger for it fades.

4. **Bitterness and Unforgiveness** – Old wounds poison your heart and block God's flow.

5. **Distant Relationship with God** – You feel disconnected, powerless, or "going through the motions."

David prayed in Psalm 51:11, **"Cast me not away from thy presence; and take not thy holy spirit from me." (KJV).** Spiritual toxins cloud intimacy with God, but awareness is the first step to renewal.

The Danger of Ignoring the Signs

When physical symptoms are ignored, sickness worsens. When spiritual signs are neglected, hearts grow cold, relationships with God fracture, and doors to the enemy open. What begins as a "small" compromise or "minor" distraction can lead to full spiritual stagnation. Hebrews 12:1 urges us to **"lay aside every weight, and the sin which doth so easily beset us, and let us run with patience the race that is set before us" (KJV).**

Detox is not optional—it is life-saving. Both the natural body and the spiritual life depend on it.

Hope for Renewal

The beauty of recognizing the signs is that they point us to hope. God has provided cleansing through:

- **His Word** (John 15:3 – **"Now ye are clean through the word which I have spoken unto you." (KJV)**).

- **The Blood of Jesus** (1 John 1:7 – **"the blood of Jesus Christ his Son cleanseth us from all sin." (KJV)**).

- **The Holy Spirit** (Titus 3:5 – **"he saved us, by the washing of regeneration, and renewing of the Holy Ghost;" (KJV)**).

What looks like heaviness can become a testimony of healing when you allow God's detoxifying power to flow through your life.

Reflection Questions

1. Do you recognize any physical, mental, or spiritual signs of toxin buildup in your own life?

2. Which of these areas—body, mind, or spirit—do you feel needs attention right now?

3. How has ignoring these signs affected your walk with God or your daily life?

Prayer

Father, I thank You for revealing the areas in my life where I need renewal. I confess that I have allowed toxins to build up—in my body, my mind, and my spirit. Today, I surrender these areas to You. Cleanse me by the blood of Jesus, renew me through Your Word, and restore me by Your Spirit. I receive Your healing, peace, and freedom. In Jesus' name. Amen.

Declaration

I declare that I will no longer ignore the warning signs in my life. I am sensitive to the Holy Spirit, and I respond quickly when God calls me to renewal. My body, mind, and spirit are cleansed and aligned with God's perfect will. I walk in freedom, health, and victory.

Part II

Spiritual Detox

Chapter 5

Detoxing the Soul – Releasing Sin, Guilt, and Shame

The soul is the seat of our emotions, thoughts, and will. When the soul is heavy, it clouds judgment, distorts perspective, and robs us of joy. Many believers live in bondage, not because God has not forgiven them, but because they are still carrying the residue of sin, guilt, and shame. Just as toxins clog the physical body, these spiritual toxins weigh down the soul, preventing freedom and intimacy with God.

Psalm 42:11 captures this struggle: **"Why art thou cast down, O my soul? and why art thou disquieted within me? hope thou in God: for I shall yet praise him, who is the health of my countenance, and my God." (KJV).** A downcast soul is a soul in need of detox—cleansing from the burdens of sin, guilt, and shame.

The Weight of Sin

Sin is the root toxin that poisons the soul. Romans 3:23 reminds us, **"For all have sinned, and come short of the glory of God;" (KJV).** Sin separates us from God, stains the conscience, and disrupts the peace of the soul. Even when forgiven, unconfessed or hidden sin can weigh heavily on the heart, producing anxiety, fear, or a sense of distance from God.

David described the burden of unconfessed sin in Psalm 32:3–4: **"When I kept silence, my bones waxed old through my roaring all the day long. For day and night thy hand was heavy upon me: my moisture is turned into the drought of summer. Selah."** **(KJV).**

The first step in detoxing the soul is confession. When we openly acknowledge sin before God, He is faithful to cleanse us (**see 1 John 1:9**). Confession is not weakness; it is the pathway to freedom.

The Poison of Guilt

While conviction from the Holy Spirit is healthy, guilt that lingers after repentance becomes toxic. Conviction draws us to God, but guilt pushes us away. Many believers live forgiven but not free because they cannot let go of the weight of their past.

Hebrews 10:22 encourages us: **"Let us draw near with a true heart in full assurance of faith, having our hearts sprinkled from an evil conscience, and our bodies washed with pure water." (KJV).**

Carrying guilt is like drinking poison and expecting healing—it destroys peace, steals joy, and clouds faith. The detox of guilt requires embracing the truth that once confessed, sins are fully forgiven. Psalm 103:12 declares: "As far as the east is from the west, so far hath he removed our transgressions from us." (KJV).

The Chains of Shame

Shame goes even deeper than guilt. While guilt says, "I did something wrong," shame whispers, "I am something wrong." Shame attacks identity, leaving believers feeling unworthy of God's love, unfit for service, or disqualified from destiny.

Adam and Eve, after sinning, hid from God because of shame (**see Genesis 3:10**). Shame leads to isolation, secrecy, and a distorted view of God's grace. But the cross of Jesus broke the power of shame. Hebrews 12:2 tells us that Jesus endured the cross, "despising the shame," so that we could walk free.

Detoxing from shame requires not only forgiveness of sins but also receiving the truth of who we are in Christ: beloved, redeemed, and chosen.

Detox Steps for the Soul

1. **Confess Sin Honestly** – Don't cover it up; lay it bare before God (**see Proverbs 28:13**).

2. **Receive Forgiveness by Faith** – Believe that Christ's sacrifice is enough (**see 1 John 1:9**).

3. **Reject Condemnation** – Remember, "There is now no condemnation for those who are in Christ Jesus" (**see Romans 8:1**).

4. **Release Shame** – Replace lies about your identity with God's truth: you are His child (**see John 1:12**).

5. **Renew Your Mind** – Meditate daily on scriptures that affirm forgiveness and freedom.

The Fruit of a Detoxed Soul

When the soul is cleansed, peace returns. Joy flows freely. Intimacy with God deepens. You no longer approach Him as a condemned sinner but as a beloved child. A detoxed soul produces a lightness, a freedom to worship, and the strength to walk in victory.

Isaiah 61:3 promises beauty for ashes, joy for mourning, and a garment of praise for the spirit of heaviness. This is the exchange God offers in the detox of the soul.

Reflection Questions

1. Are there unconfessed sins weighing on your soul right now?

2. Do you struggle more with guilt (what you did) or shame (who you believe you are)?

3. What truth from God's Word can you hold onto to replace guilt and shame with freedom?

Prayer

Father, I come before You with an open heart. I confess my sins, and I lay down the guilt and shame that have weighed on my soul. Thank You for the blood of Jesus that cleanses me fully and forever. Help me to embrace my identity as Your beloved child. Heal my soul, restore my joy, and fill me with peace. In Jesus' name. Amen.

Declaration

I declare that I am free from sin, guilt, and shame through the blood of Jesus Christ. My soul is cleansed, my identity is secure, and my spirit is restored. I walk boldly in the freedom of God's love and grace.

Chapter 6

Detoxing the Mind – Renewing Your Thoughts with the Word of God

The mind is a powerful gift from God. It shapes our perspective, influences our choices, and determines the direction of our lives. Proverbs 23:7 declares, **"For as he thinketh in his heart, so is he: Eat and drink, saith he to thee; but his heart is not with thee." (KJV).** The quality of your thoughts determines the quality of your life.

But the mind is also the place where the enemy wages his fiercest battles. He plants lies, doubts, and fears to corrupt our thinking. If left unchecked, these toxic thoughts take root and shape how we see ourselves, how we view God, and how we respond to life's challenges.

A mental detox is not just about positive thinking—it is about removing lies and replacing them with God's truth. The mind must be cleansed daily with the Word of God so that we can walk in freedom, clarity, and victory.

The Battle for the Mind

Every believer experiences the pull of competing voices—the voice of God, the lies of the enemy, and the noise of the world. Paul recognized this when he wrote:

- **"And be not conformed to this world: but be ye transformed by the renewing of your mind, that ye may prove what is that good, and acceptable, and perfect, will of God." (Romans 12:2)**

- **"Casting down imaginations, and every high thing that exalteth itself against the knowledge of God, and bringing into captivity every thought to the obedience of Christ;" (2 Corinthians 10:5)**

The enemy knows that if he can poison your thoughts, he can weaken your faith. Thoughts become beliefs, beliefs become habits, and habits become destiny. That is why mental detox is essential: to identify lies, uproot them, and replace them with the truth of God's Word.

Signs of a Toxic Mind

A mind in need of detox may show these symptoms:

1. **Negative Self-Talk** – Constantly criticizing yourself or believing you are unworthy.

2. **Fear and Anxiety** – Worrying about the future rather than trusting God's promises.

3. **Confusion and Doubt** – Struggling to discern God's will due to mental clutter.

4. **Comparison and Envy** – Measuring your worth against others.

5. **Hopelessness** – Believing your situation or life will never change.

These are not just random thoughts—they are spiritual attacks designed to steal peace, joy, and confidence.

The Word of God as the Mind's Cleanser

The most powerful tool for mental detox is the Word of God. Scripture acts as both filter and purifier:

- **Filter** – It helps us discern truth from lies (**see Hebrews 4:12**).

- **Purifier** – It washes away fear, guilt, and negativity (**see Ephesians 5:26**).

When Jesus faced temptation in the wilderness, He responded to every lie of Satan with, "It is written" (**see Matthew 4:4, 7, 10**). The mind is renewed when it is fed, filled, and saturated with God's Word.

Steps for Detoxing the Mind

1. **Identify the Lies** – Recognize recurring negative or unbiblical thoughts.

2. **Replace with Truth** – Find scripture that speaks directly to those lies. (for example: Replace "I am weak" with **"I can do all things through Christ which strengtheneth me."** – **Philippians 4:13 - KJV).**

3. **Guard the Input** – Limit exposure to toxic media, conversations, and environments that feed negative thoughts **(see Philippians 4:8)**.

4. **Practice Gratitude** – Gratitude shifts focus from what's wrong to what God has done **(see 1 Thessalonians 5:18)**.

5. **Meditate Daily** – Reflect on scripture, letting it take root in your mind **(see Joshua 1:8)**.

A Transformed Mind Produces a Transformed Life

When your mind is renewed, your entire life shifts. Peace replaces anxiety. Confidence replaces insecurity. Hope replaces despair. You begin to think with the mind of Christ **(see 1 Corinthians 2:16)**, and your decisions align with God's will.

A detoxed mind produces fruit: clarity, creativity, resilience, and faith. You no longer live as a victim of your thoughts—you live as a victor through Christ.

Reflection Questions

1. What recurring negative thoughts have you struggled with?

2. Which areas of your life have been shaped by lies rather than God's truth?

3. What scriptures can you meditate on daily to renew your mind?

Prayer

Father, I surrender my mind to You. Forgive me for allowing toxic thoughts to rule me. Expose the lies I have believed, and replace them with Your truth. Wash my mind with the power of Your Word. Renew my thoughts, align them with Your promises, and give me the mind of Christ. In Jesus' name. Amen.

Declaration

I declare that my mind is renewed by the Word of God. I reject every lie of the enemy and embrace the truth of scripture. My thoughts are aligned with God's will, my focus is clear, and my faith is strong. I have the mind of Christ, and I walk in peace and victory.

Chapter 7

Detoxing the Heart – Forgiveness, Healing, and Letting Go of Offense

The Bible tells us in Proverbs 4:23, **"Keep thy heart with all diligence; for out of it are the issues of life." (KJV).** The heart is the wellspring of life. It is where love, faith, and passion for God dwell. But it is also where pain, offense, and unforgiveness can take root. A toxic heart leads to toxic relationships, distorted thinking, and hindered fellowship with God.

Detoxing the heart is one of the most powerful and necessary steps in spiritual renewal. Without forgiveness, bitterness grows. Without healing, wounds deepen. Without releasing offense, we remain chained to the past. A detoxed heart, however, is free to love, to worship, and to walk in peace.

The Burden of Unforgiveness

Unforgiveness is like carrying a backpack full of stones—every offense adds weight until you can no longer move freely. Jesus was clear about the danger of unforgiveness: **"But if ye forgive not men their trespasses, neither will your Father forgive your trespasses." (Matthew 6:15 - KJV).**

Unforgiveness is a spiritual toxin that poisons not the offender, but the offended. It eats away at peace, joy, and health. Studies even show that bitterness and resentment can cause stress, high blood pressure, and depression. Spiritually, unforgiveness blocks prayers (**see Mark 11:25**) and hinders intimacy with God.

Detox begins when you make the decision to forgive—not because the offender deserves it, but because you deserve freedom.

The Power of Healing

A heart weighed down with wounds cannot fully love. Pain from betrayal, rejection, or broken trust lingers like toxins in the soul. David cried out in Psalm 147:3, **"He healeth the broken in heart, and bindeth up their wounds." (KJV).** Healing is God's promise, but it requires surrender.

True healing comes when we:

1. Acknowledge the hurt instead of burying it.

2. Invite God into the wound instead of self-medicating with anger or distraction.

3. Receive His love as the balm that restores.

Healing is not forgetting—it is remembering without pain. It is moving forward without carrying the infection of the past.

The Trap of Offense

Jesus warned in Luke 17:1, **"It is impossible but that offences will come: but woe unto him, through whom they come!" (KJV).**

Offenses are inevitable, but carrying them is optional. Offense is one of the enemy's most effective toxins—it hardens hearts, divides churches, and destroys relationships.

When offense is not released, it turns into bitterness. Hebrews 12:15 warns: **"Looking diligently lest any man fail of the grace of God; lest any root of bitterness springing up trouble you, and thereby many be defiled;" (KJV).** One person's offense can spread like poison if left unchecked.

Detoxing from offense requires humility. It is choosing peace over pride, reconciliation over resentment, and freedom over bondage.

Practical Steps for Heart Detox

1. **Pray for the Offender** – It's difficult to remain bitter toward those you lift up in prayer (**see Matthew 5:44**).

2. **Release the Debt** – Forgiveness means letting go of the "debt" others owe you, just as Christ forgave you (**see Ephesians 4:32**).

3. **Speak Life** – Replace harsh words with words of blessing (**see Romans 12:14**).

4. **Guard Against New Offenses** – Stay rooted in love and slow to anger (**see James 1:19–20**).

5. **Invite God's Healing Daily** – Healing the heart is not a one-time event but an ongoing process.

The Fruit of a Detoxed Heart

A cleansed heart overflows with love, peace, and joy. Worship flows freely. Relationships are restored. You walk in the lightness of God's presence, no longer chained to what others have done to you. A detoxed heart can love even enemies and forgive even the deepest wounds, reflecting the heart of Christ on the cross when He prayed, **"Father, forgive them; for they know not what they do." (Luke 23:34a - KJV).**

Reflection Questions

1. Who or what offense are you still holding in your heart?

2. How has unforgiveness or bitterness affected your spiritual growth?

3. What steps can you take today to begin detoxing your heart?

Prayer

Father, I bring my heart before You. I confess that I have held onto unforgiveness, pain, and offense. Today I choose to release every person who has hurt me. Heal the wounds of my past, bind up my brokenness, and cleanse my heart from bitterness. Fill me with Your love, peace, and joy. Create in me a pure heart, O God, and renew a steadfast spirit within me. In Jesus' name. Amen.

Declaration

I declare that my heart is free from bitterness, unforgiveness, and offense. I choose forgiveness, I receive healing, and I walk in the love of Christ. My heart is pure, my spirit is light, and my life is a reflection of God's grace.

Chapter 8

Detoxing the Spirit – Prayer, Fasting, and Worship as Cleansing Tools

T he spirit is the deepest part of who we are. It is where we connect with God, where His presence dwells, and where His voice speaks. Proverbs 20:27 says, **"The spirit of man is the candle of the Lord, searching all the inward parts of the belly." (KJV).** When the spirit is weighed down by sin, neglect, or distraction, the lamp grows dim, and clarity is lost.

Just as the body requires detox from physical toxins and the mind from negative thoughts, the spirit requires detox from spiritual pollution. This happens through three powerful tools: prayer, fasting, and worship. These are not rituals, but divine pathways that cleanse, strengthen, and revive the spirit.

Prayer: The Oxygen of the Spirit

Prayer is not just communication with God; it is communion with Him. It is the lifeline that keeps the spirit alive and vibrant. Without prayer, the spirit suffocates under the weight of worldly cares.

- **Prayer Cleanses** – Confession and intercession wash away heaviness **(see Psalm 66:18, 1 John 1:9).**

- **Prayer Renews** – In God's presence, strength is exchanged for weakness (**see Isaiah 40:31**).

- **Prayer Protects** – It builds a shield against spiritual attacks (**see Ephesians 6:18**).

A spirit in detox uses prayer to pour out burdens and receive the refreshing of God's presence. Prayer is where toxins of worry, anger, and fear are released, and peace is restored.

Fasting: The Discipline that Breaks Chains

Fasting is one of the most powerful spiritual detox tools. It is the act of denying the flesh to strengthen the spirit. Jesus Himself fasted for forty days before beginning His ministry (**see Matthew 4:1– 11**), and He taught that certain breakthroughs come only through prayer and fasting (**see Matthew 17:21**).

- **Fasting Purifies Motives** – It strips away reliance on comfort and reveals where our dependence lies.

- **Fasting Breaks Strongholds** – Isaiah 58:6 declares, **"Is not this the fast that I have chosen? to loose the bands of wickedness, to undo the heavy burdens, and to let the oppressed go free, and that ye break every yoke?"**

- **Fasting Increases Sensitivity** – It silences the noise of the flesh so the spirit can hear clearly.

Natural detox removes toxins from the body; spiritual fasting removes toxins from the soul. Together, they sharpen discernment and restore intimacy with God.

Worship: The Atmosphere of Cleansing

Worship is more than singing songs—it is the posture of a surrendered heart. When we worship, we create an atmosphere where toxins cannot remain. Depression, fear, and oppression dissolve in the presence of God's glory.

1. **Worship Shifts Focus** – From problems to the greatness of God (**see Psalm 34:3**).

2. **Worship Cleanses the Spirit** – It replaces heaviness with a garment of praise (**see Isaiah 61:3**).

3. **Worship Heals and Restores** – Saul's tormenting spirit left when David worshiped on the harp (**see 1 Samuel 16:23**).

A worshipping spirit is a detoxed spirit. It is light, free, and filled with joy.

The Threefold Cord of Detox

Prayer, fasting, and worship are powerful individually, but together they form a threefold cord of spiritual cleansing.

- Prayer aligns the heart with God.
- Fasting silences the flesh.
- Worship fills the spirit with God's presence.

This combination not only removes toxins but also fortifies the believer against future contamination.

Practical Steps for Spiritual Detox

1. **Set Aside Daily Time** – Commit to consistent prayer, even if brief, to reset the spirit.

2. **Begin with Simple Fasting** – Skip one meal or a particular food, using that time for prayer.

3. **Create a Worship Atmosphere** – Fill your home or car with worship music and cultivate praise.

4. **Journal Your Encounters** – Record prayers, revelations, and scriptures during your detox.

5. **Stay Accountable** – Invite a prayer partner to join you in fasting or intercession.

The Fruit of a Detoxed Spirit

A spirit cleansed by prayer, fasting, and worship is marked by:

- Greater clarity in hearing God's voice.
- Stronger resistance against temptation.
- A renewed hunger for the Word.
- Overflowing peace and joy.
- Fresh anointing for service and ministry.

Psalm 51:10 captures the cry of a detoxed spirit: **"Create in me a clean heart, O God; and renew a right spirit within me." (KJV).**

Reflection Questions

1. What role does prayer currently play in your daily spiritual health?

2. Have you experienced the cleansing power of fasting? If so, how?

3. How could worship become a more intentional part of your lifestyle, not just a Sunday activity?

Prayer

Father, I present my spirit before You. Cleanse me through the power of prayer, sharpen me through the discipline of fasting, and fill me with joy through the beauty of worship. Remove every toxin of sin, fear, or distraction that dulls my spirit. Renew my passion for Your presence and restore my hunger for You. In Jesus' name. Amen.

Declaration

I declare that my spirit is alive and refreshed in God's presence. Through prayer, I am strengthened. Through fasting, I am purified. Through worship, I am filled with joy. I walk in clarity, freedom, and power by the Spirit of the Lord.

Chapter 9

Breaking Strongholds and Spiritual Addictions

While prayer, fasting, and worship cleanse the spirit, many believers still wrestle with strongholds—deeply rooted patterns of thinking and behavior that resist change. A stronghold is not just a bad habit; it is a fortified place in the mind or spirit where the enemy has gained influence. Left unchallenged, strongholds and spiritual addictions can dominate lives, distort identity, and derail purpose.

But the good news is this: God has given us divine power to demolish strongholds. 2 Corinthians 10:4 declares, **"(For the weapons of our warfare are not carnal, but mighty through God to the pulling down of strong holds;)" (KJV).** Spiritual detox means not just cleansing surface-level toxins but also breaking chains that have held us captive.

What Are Strongholds?

A stronghold is a lie the enemy convinces you to believe, reinforced by repeated behavior. Over time, it becomes a fortress in your mind or spirit.

Strongholds often include:

- Addictions (pornography, drugs, alcohol, gambling, etc.).
- Cycles of fear or worry.
- Pride and self-reliance.
- Generational patterns of sin (anger, poverty, immorality).
- Unforgiveness and bitterness.

The danger of a stronghold is that it feels permanent. But no fortress of the enemy is stronger than the power of Christ.

The Nature of Spiritual Addictions

Spiritual addictions go beyond physical cravings; they are compulsions of the soul and spirit. They can look like:

- **Approval Addiction** – Needing constant validation from others.

- **Emotional Addiction** – Holding onto anger, drama, or self-pity because it feels familiar.

- **Religious Addiction** – Performing rituals for acceptance instead of living by grace.

- **Digital/Worldly Addiction** – Being enslaved to entertainment, social media, or materialism.

Jesus said, **"Whosoever committeth sin is the servant of sin. If the Son therefore shall make you free, ye shall be free indeed." (John 8:34, 36 - KJV).** Detox is not complete until these hidden addictions are broken.

Steps to Breaking Strongholds

1. **Identify the Stronghold** – Name the pattern. You cannot cast down what you refuse to confront. (**see Psalm 139:23–24**).

2. **Renounce the Lie** – Replace it with God's truth. Example: Replace "I will always be bound" with "Where the Spirit of the Lord is, there is freedom" (**see 2 Corinthians 3:17**).

3. **Use the Word as a Weapon** – Speak scripture over the area of bondage. (**see Ephesians 6:17**).

4. **Engage in Fasting and Prayer** – Some strongholds only break with this level of spiritual discipline (**see Mark 9:29**).

5. **Stay Accountable** – Healing happens in community. Confess struggles to trusted believers (**see James 5:16**).

6. **Walk in Daily Surrender** – Deliverance is both an event and a process. You must renew your commitment to freedom daily.

Biblical Examples of Stronghold-Breaking

- **Gideon** – Delivered Israel after breaking down his father's altar to Baal (**see Judges 6:25–27**).

- **Paul** – Transformed from persecutor of the church to preacher of the gospel after encountering Christ (**see Acts 9**).

- **Mary Magdalene** – Delivered from seven demons and became a faithful follower of Jesus (**see Luke 8:2**).

Each story reminds us that no bondage is too strong for God's power.

Signs of Deliverance and Freedom

You know a stronghold is breaking when:

- Desires that once controlled you begin to lose their grip.

- Peace and clarity replace confusion and oppression.

- You find joy in God's presence instead of worldly substitutes.

- Old temptations no longer dominate your decisions.

John 8:36 rings true: **"If the Son therefore shall make you free, ye shall be free indeed." (KJV).**

The Fruit of a Detoxed Spirit Free from Strongholds

When strongholds are broken, spiritual addictions lose their grip. You step into freedom, clarity, and authority. You no longer walk as a slave, but as a child of God. You discover new strength to resist temptation, new joy in God's presence, and new boldness in fulfilling your purpose.

Reflection Questions

1. What strongholds or addictions have you struggled with that feel difficult to break?

2. What lies have you believed that God wants to replace with His truth?

3. Who can walk with you as an accountability partner on your journey to freedom?

Prayer

Lord, I bring before You every stronghold and addiction in my life. I renounce the lies I have believed, and I declare that Your truth sets me free. Break every chain that has bound me, silence every voice of the enemy, and fill me with Your Spirit. Strengthen me to walk daily in freedom, victory, and purity. In Jesus' name. Amen.

Declaration

I declare that every stronghold in my life is demolished by the power of God. I am no longer a slave to sin, fear, or addiction. I walk in freedom, I live in victory, and I am empowered by the Holy Spirit to fulfill my purpose.

Chapter 10

Maintaining a Clean Spirit – Daily Habits for Purity and Growth

D etox is not just a one-time event—it is a lifestyle. Just as eating one healthy meal or drinking water for a single day won't permanently cleanse the body, a single act of prayer or repentance won't sustain spiritual purity. The goal is not only to experience freedom but to remain free.

Jesus warned in Matthew 12:43–45 that when an unclean spirit leaves a person, it seeks to return. If the heart is left "empty," the person may end up worse than before. This shows us that maintaining a clean spirit requires continual filling, guarding, and growth. A detoxed spirit must be nurtured daily to stay strong and pure.

Guarding the Gateways

Your spirit is influenced by what enters through your eyes, ears, and heart. Proverbs 4:23 instructs: **"Keep thy heart with all diligence; for out of it are the issues of life." (KJV).**

- **Eyes** – Be mindful of what you watch or read. Images and words can plant seeds of purity or corruption.

- **Ears** – Choose carefully the conversations, music, and voices you allow to shape your thoughts.

- **Heart** – Keep it free from bitterness, envy, and pride. Invite the Holy Spirit to search it daily (**see Psalm 139:23–24**).

Guarding these gateways is a daily act of stewardship over your spiritual health.

Daily Spiritual Habits for Purity

1. **Consistent Prayer** – Begin and end each day in communion with God (**see 1 Thessalonians 5:17**). Prayer keeps the spirit sensitive and uncluttered.

2. **Daily Scripture Intake** – Let God's Word wash and renew your mind. Even a few verses meditated on daily bring cleansing (**see John 15:3**).

3. **Regular Worship** – Make worship a lifestyle, not just a Sunday activity. Praise drives out heaviness and keeps the spirit free (**see Isaiah 61:3**).

4. **Confession and Repentance** – Don't allow sin to pile up. Confess quickly and walk in grace (**see 1 John 1:9**).

5. **Fasting in Rhythm** – Incorporate fasting as a discipline, not only in crisis. It keeps the flesh in check and the spirit sharp.

Staying in Fellowship

Isolation is one of the easiest ways for toxins to re-enter the spirit. Hebrews 10:25 urges, **"Do not give up meeting together… but encourage one another."** Fellowship with other believers provides accountability, encouragement, and mutual sharpening (**see Proverbs 27:17**).

When you surround yourself with others pursuing purity, your spirit is strengthened. Fellowship creates an atmosphere where toxins are less likely to take root.

Living with Sensitivity to the Holy Spirit

The Holy Spirit is your internal "detox monitor." He convicts, warns, and guides when something is contaminating your spirit. Ephesians 4:30 reminds us: **"And grieve not the holy Spirit of God, whereby ye are sealed unto the day of redemption." (KJV).** Maintaining a clean spirit requires listening to His promptings—turning away from things that pollute and embracing the things that bring life.

The Discipline of Rest

Spiritual detox is not only about doing more, but also about resting in God. Rest allows the spirit to reset, to receive, and to abide in His presence. Jesus often withdrew to lonely places to pray (**see Luke 5:16**). In the same way, making time for quiet reflection and rest is vital for long-term purity.

Signs of a Spirit Remaining Clean

You know your spirit is being maintained when you experience:

- Ongoing peace, even in storms (**see Philippians 4:7**).
- Consistent hunger for God's Word.
- Greater sensitivity to sin and conviction.
- Joy in prayer and worship.
- Increasing fruit of the Spirit—love, joy, peace, patience, kindness, goodness, faithfulness, gentleness, and self-control (**see Galatians 5:22–23**).

Reflection Questions

1. Which daily habit do you need to strengthen most—prayer, Word, worship, confession, or fasting?

2. What "gateways" in your life (eyes, ears, heart) need greater guarding?

3. How can you create a spiritual rhythm that keeps your spirit clean and vibrant?

Prayer

Lord, I thank You for the freedom and cleansing You have brought into my life. Help me to maintain a clean spirit daily. Teach me to guard my heart, to stay rooted in Your Word, to pray without ceasing, and to live in constant worship. May my life remain a vessel of purity and a temple for Your Spirit. Keep me sensitive to Your voice and strong in Your presence. In Jesus' name. Amen.

Declaration

I declare that I will live with a clean spirit. I will guard my heart, fill my mind with God's Word, and keep my life anchored in prayer and worship. I walk daily in purity, strength, and growth. My spirit is alive, my heart is guarded, and my life glorifies God.

Part III

Natural Detox

Chapter 11

The Body as God's Temple – Why Physical Health Matters

When most people hear the word "detox," they think first of the body—cleansing from processed foods, harmful substances, or environmental toxins. While the physical aspect is important, as believers, we must understand that our bodies are not just physical vessels but spiritual temples.

Paul declares in 1 Corinthians 6:19–20, **"What? know ye not that your body is the temple of the Holy Ghost which is in you, which ye have of God, and ye are not your own? For ye are bought with a price: therefore glorify God in your body, and in your spirit, which are God's." (KJV).** This verse frames the foundation of natural detox. Taking care of our physical health is not vanity, but an act of worship.

The Body as God's Temple

In the Old Testament, the temple was sacred. It was carefully cleansed, maintained, and honored as the dwelling place of God's presence. Now, under the New Covenant, our physical bodies serve as the temple. If God's Spirit dwells in us, then what we consume, how we treat our bodies, and how we manage our health reflect our reverence for Him.

When the temple is neglected or defiled, worship is hindered. Likewise, when our bodies are overwhelmed with toxins—whether from poor diet, lack of exercise, or harmful habits—our spiritual service is weakened. A body that is constantly sick, fatigued, or weighed down cannot serve God with full strength.

Why Physical Health Matters Spiritually

1. **Clarity of Spirit** – A healthy body supports a clear and focused mind, making it easier to pray, worship, and discern God's voice.

2. **Energy for Service** – Kingdom work requires strength. A body burdened by toxins or poor health struggles to fulfill God's assignments.

3. **Witness to the World** – Caring for your body reflects stewardship and discipline, which speaks to others about the God you serve.

4. **Longevity of Purpose** – A healthy lifestyle allows you to live longer and accomplish more for God's kingdom.

Romans 12:1 reminds us: **"I beseech you therefore, brethren, by the mercies of God, that ye present your bodies a living sacrifice, holy, acceptable unto God, which is your reasonable service." (KJV).** Natural detox is therefore a form of consecration—bringing even our physical health under God's Lordship.

The Consequences of Neglecting the Temple

Just as neglecting a physical temple leads to ruin, neglecting our health leads to breakdown. Poor diet, lack of rest, constant stress, and exposure to harmful substances open the door to disease, fatigue, and even premature death. Hosea 4:6 declares, **"My people are destroyed for lack of knowledge:" (KJV).** Many believers suffer simply because they do not recognize that what they eat, drink, or expose themselves to impacts their spiritual effectiveness.

Neglecting the temple:

- Weakens physical stamina.
- Clouds mental focus.
- Opens doors to unnecessary illness.
- Shortens the ability to carry out purpose.

Natural Detox as Stewardship

Detoxing the body is not about chasing diet trends or extremes; it is about stewardship. God entrusts us with our physical health, and we must steward it wisely. Choosing water over soda, vegetables over processed foods, and rest over constant work is not legalism—it is worship.

1 Corinthians 10:31 says, **"Whether therefore ye eat, or drink, or whatsoever ye do, do all to the glory of God." (KJV).** When you detox naturally, you are honoring God with even the smallest daily choices.

Practical Ways to Begin Treating Your Body as God's Temple

1. **Hydrate Properly** – Water flushes toxins and refreshes the body. Aim to drink consistently throughout the day.

2. **Eat Whole Foods** – Prioritize fruits, vegetables, whole grains, and lean proteins. Reduce processed and chemical-laden foods.

3. **Rest Intentionally** – Sleep restores the body and allows healing. **(see Psalm 127:2)**.

4. **Move Your Body** – Exercise strengthens the temple and supports longevity.

5. **Limit Harmful Intake** – Detox from substances like excess sugar, caffeine, alcohol, or anything addictive.

6. **Practice Moderation** – Gluttony and neglect are both forms of dishonoring the temple. Balance is key.

The Spiritual Parallel

Every time you make a healthy choice for your body, it reflects a spiritual reality: cleansing, discipline, and alignment with God's will. Natural detox parallels spiritual detox because both are about removing what hinders and restoring what gives life.

The Fruit of Honoring the Temple

When you care for your body as God's temple, you experience:

- Greater energy and vitality.
- Clearer focus for prayer and study.
- Stronger immunity and resilience.
- A greater sense of alignment between spirit, soul, and body.

Honoring your body is not about perfection; it is about obedience and gratitude for the vessel God gave you.

Reflection Questions

1. How have you viewed your body—as a temporary shell or as God's temple?

2. What physical habits (food, rest, exercise) are hindering your ability to serve God with full strength?

3. What small changes can you make this week to begin honoring God with your health?

Prayer

Lord, I thank You for creating my body as a temple for Your Spirit. Forgive me for the ways I have neglected or abused this temple. Teach me to steward my health with wisdom and discipline. Help me to make choices that honor You—what I eat, drink, and how I rest. Strengthen me so that I can serve You fully with energy, clarity, and devotion. In Jesus' name. Amen.

Declaration

I declare that my body is the temple of the Holy Spirit. I will honor God with my health, my habits, and my lifestyle. I choose cleansing over toxins, discipline over neglect, and stewardship over waste. My body, mind, and spirit are aligned to glorify God.

Chapter 12

Nutrition for Cleansing – Foods That Heal and Restore

Food is more than fuel—it is medicine, it is stewardship, and it is a reflection of God's design. From the beginning, God provided food, not just for survival but for health and vitality. Genesis 1:29 says, **"And God said, Behold, I have given you every herb bearing seed, which is upon the face of all the earth, and every tree, in the which is the fruit of a tree yielding seed; to you it shall be for meat." (KJV).**

When we eat in alignment with God's design, our bodies thrive. But when we fill ourselves with processed, artificial, and chemical-laden foods, toxins accumulate, energy diminishes, and illness finds an open door. Nutrition plays a vital role in detoxifying the body and keeping the temple of the Holy Spirit strong.

God's Original Design for Food

In the Garden of Eden, man's first meals were plant-based: fruits, vegetables, nuts, and grains. These foods were nutrient-rich, natural, and healing. Daniel demonstrated this when he refused the king's rich food and instead ate vegetables and water for ten days. The Bible records that "they looked healthier and better nourished than any of the young men who ate the royal food" (**see Daniel 1:15**).

This example shows that God's original food plan is still effective for restoring health and vitality. Natural, whole foods carry healing properties that processed foods cannot replicate.

Foods That Heal and Restore

When embarking on a natural detox, prioritize foods that cleanse, nourish, and strengthen the body:

1. **Fruits** – Rich in antioxidants, vitamins, and fiber. Apples cleanse the liver, berries fight inflammation, and citrus fruits flush toxins.

2. **Vegetables** – Leafy greens like spinach, kale, and broccoli alkalize the body and strengthen immunity. Cruciferous vegetables (cabbage, cauliflower) support liver detox.

3. **Whole Grains** – Brown rice, quinoa, oats, and barley provide fiber for digestion and steady energy.

4. **Legumes** – Beans and lentils support cleansing by stabilizing blood sugar and providing plant-based protein.

5. **Nuts and Seeds** – Almonds, walnuts, chia seeds, and flaxseeds provide healthy fats, supporting brain and heart health.

6. **Herbs and Spices** – Turmeric, ginger, garlic, and parsley have anti-inflammatory and cleansing properties.

7. **Water** – Not food, but the most vital detox agent. It flushes toxins, hydrates cells, and restores energy.

Foods That Harm and Pollute

Just as some foods heal, others poison. These are modern "toxins" that often lead to sluggishness, inflammation, and long-term illness:

- **Excess Sugar** – Fuels disease, causes cravings, and weakens immunity.

- **Processed Foods** – Laden with preservatives, chemicals, and artificial flavors.

- **Excess Salt** – Leads to bloating, dehydration, and high blood pressure.

- **Refined Grains** – White bread, pasta, and pastries spike blood sugar and provide little nutrition.

- **Unhealthy Fats** – Trans fats and fried foods clog arteries and slow digestion.

- **Overconsumption** – Gluttony, even of "good" foods, burdens the body.

1 Corinthians 6:12 warns, **"All things are lawful unto me, but all things are not expedient: all things are lawful for me, but I will not be brought under the power of any." (KJV).** Food must serve us, not master us.

The Spiritual Connection

Nutrition impacts not only the body but also the spirit. Poor diet leads to fatigue, irritability, and lack of focus, which weakens prayer and devotion. A nourished body, on the other hand, gives strength for worship, service, and fulfilling purpose.

Eating clean parallels spiritual purity:

- Just as natural food detoxifies, the Word of God cleanses the soul.

- Just as harmful foods pollute the body, sinful influences pollute the spirit.

- Just as balance in diet sustains health, balance in spiritual disciplines sustains growth.

Practical Steps for Nutritional Detox

1. **Incorporate More Plants** – Aim to fill half your plate with fruits and vegetables.

2. **Hydrate Constantly** – Drink at least 6–8 glasses of water daily. Add lemon for cleansing.

3. **Choose Whole Over Processed** – Select whole grains, natural proteins, and raw snacks over packaged foods.

4. **Use Food as Medicine** – Add garlic for immunity, ginger for digestion, and turmeric for inflammation.

5. **Practice Moderation** – Enjoy balance instead of extremes—discipline, not deprivation.

The Fruit of Eating God's Way

When you align your diet with God's natural provision, you experience:

- More energy and vitality for daily living.
- Stronger immunity and quicker recovery from illness.
- Mental clarity and sharper focus.
- Emotional stability and improved mood.
- A deeper sense of alignment between physical health and spiritual life.

Reflection Questions

1. How have your eating habits affected your energy, mood, and spiritual focus?

2. What foods in your current diet are helping your body, and which are harming it?

3. What one change can you make this week to bring your nutrition more in line with God's design?

Prayer

Father, I thank You for providing food to nourish, heal, and sustain me. Forgive me for the times I have neglected or abused this gift. Teach me to make wise choices that honor my body as Your temple.

Help me to use food not as an idol, but as a tool for strength and service. May my diet reflect discipline, gratitude, and stewardship. In Jesus' name. Amen.

Declaration

I declare that I will honor God with my food choices. My body will be fueled by what heals and restores, not what harms and pollutes. I choose discipline over indulgence, stewardship over neglect, and life-giving nutrition over empty toxins. My body is strengthened, my mind is clear, and my spirit is aligned with God.

Chapter 13

Fasting and Its Benefits – Natural and Spiritual Renewal

F asting is one of the most powerful tools for detoxifying both body and spirit. In the natural, it gives the body a chance to rest, repair, and release accumulated toxins. In the spiritual, it sharpens discernment, breaks strongholds, and draws us closer to God. Jesus Himself assumed fasting would be a part of our walk with Him. In Matthew 6:16, He said, **"When you fast..."**—not "if you fast."

Fasting is not a punishment for the body but a discipline for the soul. It is the intentional denial of food or certain pleasures for a period of time in order to realign the body, soul, and spirit with God's will. When practiced with prayer and devotion, fasting becomes a powerful act of spiritual warfare, renewal, and healing.

The Natural Benefits of Fasting

Modern science confirms what scripture and ancient practices have long testified: fasting brings tremendous benefits to the body.

1. Cleansing and Detoxification

When food is withheld for a period, the digestive system takes a break, allowing the body to focus on flushing out stored toxins and repairing damaged cells.

2. Improved Digestion

Fasting resets the digestive system, improving nutrient absorption and reducing inflammation in the gut.

3. Increased Energy and Mental Clarity

Contrary to the belief that fasting weakens the body, many report improved focus and vitality, as the body uses energy more efficiently.

4. Weight Balance and Metabolism Reset

Fasting reduces insulin resistance, balances blood sugar, and helps regulate a healthy weight.

5. Immune System Strengthening

Studies reveal that fasting triggers cellular regeneration, strengthening immunity, and reducing the risk of chronic illness.

The Spiritual Benefits of Fasting

While natural benefits are significant, the true purpose of fasting is spiritual transformation.

1. Clarity and Sensitivity to God's Voice

By quieting the noise of the flesh, fasting helps the spirit hear God more clearly. Acts 13:2 records that the early church heard the Holy Spirit's instructions while fasting and praying.

2. Breaking Strongholds

Jesus said, **"this kind goeth not out but by prayer and fasting."** **(Matthew 17:21 - KJV).** Fasting breaks spiritual barriers and generational chains.

3. Humility Before God

Psalm 35:13 says, **"I humbled my soul with fasting." (KJV).** Fasting is an act of surrender and humility, showing God that we depend on Him more than our appetites.

4. Revival of the Inner Man

Fasting revives prayer, sharpens faith, and rekindles passion for God's presence. It cleanses the spirit the way detox cleanses the body.

5. Empowerment for Spiritual Battles

Jesus began His public ministry with a 40-day fast (**see Luke 4:1– 2**). Through fasting, He overcame temptation and emerged in power, ready to minister.

Types of Fasting

Not all fasting looks the same. God may call you to different types in different seasons:

- **Complete Fast** – Abstaining from all food, drinking only water for a set period.

- **Partial Fast** – Restricting certain foods (like Daniel's fast of vegetables and water).

- **Intermittent Fast** – Eating only during set times of the day, allowing extended fasting windows.

- **Soul Fast** – Abstaining from non-food indulgences (such as social media, TV, or entertainment) to focus on God.

The key is obedience to the leading of the Holy Spirit.

Biblical Examples of Fasting

- Moses fasted 40 days on Mount Sinai and received the Ten Commandments (**see Exodus 34:28**).

- Daniel fasted and received wisdom, visions, and answered prayers (**see Daniel 9:3, 10:3**).

- Esther called her people to fast, and God used her to save Israel (**see Esther 4:16**).

- Jesus fasted 40 days and overcame Satan's temptations (**see Matthew 4:2**).

Every time fasting appears in scripture, it precedes breakthrough, revelation, or deliverance.

Practical Guidelines for Fasting

1. **Prepare Physically and Spiritually** – Don't jump into a long fast without prayer and preparation. Start small if you are new.

2. **Stay Hydrated** – Drink plenty of water or herbal teas during fasting.

3. **Replace Meals with Prayer** – Use mealtimes for Bible reading, worship, and journaling.

4. **Avoid Legalism** – Fasting is not about impressing God but drawing near to Him with humility.

5. **Break the Fast Wisely** – End gradually with light, nourishing foods.

Fasting as a Spiritual Detox

Fasting is God's reset button for the soul. It:

- Cleanses bitterness, anger, and unforgiveness.
- Restores spiritual hunger and dependency on God.
- Replaces worldly cravings with a hunger for righteousness.

Isaiah 58:6 says, **"Is not this the fast that I have chosen? to loose the bands of wickedness, to undo the heavy burdens, and to let the oppressed go free, and that ye break every yoke?" (KJV).** True fasting doesn't just benefit us; it overflows to bless others.

Reflection Questions

1. How do you view fasting—discipline, burden, or privilege?

2. When was the last time you fasted, and what was the outcome?

3. What area of your life could benefit from a season of fasting and prayer right now?

Prayer

Lord, I thank You for the gift of fasting. Teach me to approach it not as a ritual, but as a holy invitation into Your presence. Strengthen me to deny my flesh so that my spirit may rise in power. Use fasting to cleanse my body, sharpen my focus, and break every chain in my life. As I humble myself, may Your Spirit fill me with wisdom, breakthrough, and renewal. In Jesus' name. Amen.

Declaration

I declare that fasting will not weaken me but strengthen me. As I set aside food and distractions, I make room for God's presence and power. Every stronghold is broken, every chain is loosed, and every spiritual fog is lifted. My body is renewed, my mind is clear, and my spirit is on fire for God.

Chapter 14

Prayer and Meditation – Detoxing the Mind and Spirit

If fasting detoxes the body and spirit, then prayer and meditation detox the mind and soul. The mind is the battlefield where toxic thoughts, lies, and spiritual attacks often take root. Without cleansing the mind through prayer and meditation on God's Word, a person can remain in bondage, even after natural detoxification. Prayer is communication with God, while meditation is concentration on His truth. Together, they become powerful tools of renewal and freedom.

Paul wrote, **"And be not conformed to this world: but be ye transformed by the renewing of your mind, that ye may prove what is that good, and acceptable, and perfect, will of God."** **(Romans 12:2 - KJV).** Prayer and meditation are God's method of renewal. They wash away anxiety, confusion, and lies of the enemy, replacing them with truth, peace, and clarity.

The Power of Prayer in Detoxing the Spirit

Prayer is not just talking to God—it is an exchange. We bring our burdens, sins, and fears, and He gives us forgiveness, peace, and strength.

1. Prayer Removes Toxic Burdens

Jesus invites us in Matthew 11:28, **"Come unto me, all ye that labour and are heavy laden, and I will give you rest." (KJV).** Through prayer, we cast off bitterness, resentment, and emotional toxins that poison the heart.

2. Prayer Renews the Mind

Toxic thoughts often linger because we rehearse pain and rehearse offense. But in prayer, God replaces destructive thought patterns with His truth (**see Philippians 4:6–7**).

3. Prayer Strengthens the Spirit

Prayer is a spiritual detox that strengthens resilience. Just as the body becomes healthier after cleansing, the spirit becomes stronger after consistent prayer.

Meditation as a Spiritual Detox

Biblical meditation is not about emptying the mind (as in some Eastern practices), but about filling it with God's Word.

1. Meditating on God's Word

Psalm 1:2 describes the blessed person as one who **"delight...in the law of the Lord; and in his law doth he meditate day and night." (KJV).** Meditation plants God's truth deep in our hearts, flushing out lies and negativity.

2. Rewiring Toxic Thought Patterns

Scientific studies show that meditation reduces stress, improves brain function, and creates new mental pathways. Spiritually, meditating on God's promises rewires the brain to focus on hope and faith rather than fear and despair.

3. Stillness Before God

Detox requires stillness. Psalm 46:10 says, **"Be still, and know that I am God." (KJV).** Meditation trains us to quiet distractions, sit in His presence, and allow His Spirit to cleanse our inner man.

The Mind–Body–Spirit Connection

Prayer and meditation affect not only the spirit but also the body. Stress, worry, and fear release toxins in the body that weaken immunity and health. When the mind is renewed through prayer and meditation:

- Cortisol (the stress hormone) lowers.
- Sleep improves.
- Blood pressure stabilizes.
- The body functions in greater alignment with peace.

God designed our thoughts to impact our health. Proverbs 17:22 reminds us, **"A merry heart doeth good like a medicine: but a broken spirit drieth the bones." (KJV).**

Biblical Examples of Detox Through Prayer and Meditation

- **David** – Meditated on God's Word daily, which strengthened him even in times of despair (**see Psalm 119:15**).

- **Daniel** – Prayed three times a day, keeping his spirit pure, even in a pagan culture (**see Daniel 6:10**).

- **Jesus** – Withdrew often to pray in solitude, detoxing His spirit and preparing for ministry (**see Mark 1:35**).

- **Paul and Silas** – In prison, they prayed and sang hymns, releasing the toxins of fear and despair, and God shook the foundations of their captivity (**see Acts 16:25–26**).

Practical Steps for Detoxing Through Prayer and Meditation

1. **Set a Daily Time** – Begin with a consistent prayer schedule, even if short.

2. **Create a Prayer Journal** – Writing out prayers and answered petitions helps cleanse emotional buildup.

3. **Meditate on Scripture** – Choose one verse daily, repeating it aloud, pondering its meaning, and applying it.

4. **Practice Deep Breathing in Prayer** – Inhale God's peace, exhale stress and burdens.

5. **Stay Persistent** – Prayer and meditation must become lifestyle habits, not occasional acts.

Prayer and Meditation as Warfare

Detox is not passive—it's warfare. The enemy wants to fill our minds with doubt, fear, lust, and lies. Prayer and meditation dismantle his schemes.

- Prayer pulls down strongholds (**see 2 Corinthians 10:4–5**).
- Meditation builds spiritual fortitude and renews courage.
- Together, they arm believers with peace in the midst of chaos.

Reflection Questions

1. What thoughts or emotions feel like toxins in your spirit right now?

2. How consistent is your prayer life, and what changes could you make?

3. Which scripture verse could you meditate on this week to bring renewal and cleansing?

Prayer

Heavenly Father, I come before You today asking for a cleansing of my mind and spirit. Remove every toxic thought, every lie, and every heavy burden that is not of You. Wash me with the water of Your Word. Teach me to delight in prayer and to meditate on Your truth daily. Let my mind be transformed, my spirit renewed, and my life filled with peace. In Jesus' name. Amen.

Declaration

I declare that my mind is free from the toxins of fear, doubt, and negativity. Through prayer, I release burdens and receive peace. Through meditation on God's Word, I am renewed daily. My thoughts are aligned with truth, my spirit is strengthened, and my life reflects the joy of the Lord.

Chapter 15

Worship as a Form of Detox – Cleansing Through Praise

While prayer and meditation purify the heart and mind, worship and praise bring a deeper cleansing that touches the soul's core. Worship is not just singing songs—it is surrender, intimacy, and connection with God. True worship detoxes the soul by shifting our focus from self, struggles, and toxins of life to the greatness of God. Praise lifts burdens, breaks chains, and opens the way for healing.

David understood this when he wrote, **"Bless the Lord, O my soul, and forget not all his benefits: Who forgiveth all thine iniquities; who healeth all thy diseases;" (Psalm 103:2–3 - KJV).** Worship calls the soul to remember God's goodness, which flushes out despair, heaviness, and negativity.

Worship as Spiritual Cleansing

1. Worship Breaks Chains of Bondage

Worship is powerful because it invites God's presence. In His presence, toxins of fear, shame, and despair cannot remain. Acts 16:25–26 shows Paul and Silas worshiping in prison—chains fell, and doors opened. Worship detoxes oppression and brings freedom.

2. Worship Restores the Soul

When life feels heavy, worship renews joy. Psalm 22:3 reminds us that God inhabits the praises of His people. His presence becomes the cleansing agent that restores strength and refreshes the weary soul.

3. Worship Shifts the Atmosphere

Toxic environments—whether in homes, workplaces, or even within our minds—are transformed by worship. Praise invites the Spirit of God to dominate the space, displacing confusion, heaviness, and negativity.

Praise as a Weapon Against Spiritual Toxins

Praise is not passive—it is a weapon. Toxic spirits of depression, fear, and anxiety cannot withstand the sound of praise.

- **Jehoshaphat's Army** – When surrounded by enemies, Judah sent singers ahead of the battle. As they praised, God set ambushes against their enemies (**see 2 Chronicles 20:21–22**).

- **David and Saul** – When Saul was tormented by an evil spirit, David played worship, and the spirit left him (**see 1 Samuel 16:23**).

- **Joshua and Jericho** – The walls of Jericho fell after the people shouted in praise (**see Joshua 6:20**).

Each instance shows that worship does more than uplift—it cleanses atmospheres, breaks demonic oppression, and removes spiritual toxins.

Worship Detoxes the Heart from Pride and Self-Focus

The greatest toxin of the human soul is pride—self-dependence, self-glory, and self-obsession. Worship shifts the gaze back to God, dethroning pride and enthroning Him. Isaiah's vision in Isaiah 6:1–5 shows how encountering God in worship caused him to cry out, **"Woe is me, for I am undone!"** In worship, we see ourselves rightly, and God purges our hearts with His holiness.

The Healing Flow of Worship

Worship does not just cleanse the spirit; it has tangible effects on the body and emotions:

- Reduces stress and anxiety.
- Elevates mood through joy.
- Releases tension and promotes peace.
- Improves physical health by calming the nervous system.

When we worship, we align with heaven's rhythm, and toxins of stress are flushed away by supernatural peace.

The Lifestyle of Worship

Worship is not confined to Sunday services or music. True worship is a lifestyle of reverence, obedience, and gratitude. Romans 12:1 declares, **"I beseech you therefore, brethren, by the mercies of**

God, that ye present your bodies a living sacrifice, holy, acceptable unto God, which is your reasonable service." (KJV).

Detox happens not only when we sing but when we live daily in worship—choosing to obey God, walk in purity, and honor Him in all we do.

Practical Steps to Worship as Detox

1. **Start Each Day with Praise** – Begin mornings with worship instead of worry.

2. **Sing Aloud at Home** – Fill your atmosphere with worship music that lifts the spirit.

3. **Dance Before the Lord** – Physical movement in praise releases joy and breaks heaviness.

4. **Keep a Gratitude Journal** – Write daily what you thank God for—gratitude detoxes ingratitude.

5. **Worship in Spirit and Truth** – Go beyond songs; let worship flow from a surrendered heart (**see John 4:24**).

Reflection Questions

1. How do you respond when you feel heavy or burdened—do you turn to worship or to worry?

2. What toxins of pride, fear, or discouragement have worship removed in your life before?

3. How can you build a lifestyle of worship that detoxes you daily?

Prayer

Lord, I surrender to You in worship. Cleanse me of every toxin of fear, pride, and despair. I invite Your presence into my life through praise. Let my worship break every chain, heal my heart, and shift every toxic atmosphere around me. May my life become a living sacrifice of worship to You. In Jesus' name. Amen.

Declaration

I declare that worship is my weapon, my cleansing flow, and my source of renewal. Through praise, chains are broken and toxins are removed. I will worship in spirit and in truth, and my life will be filled with the presence of God.

Part IV

Living a Detoxed Life

Chapter 16

The Power of Forgiveness – Detoxing the Heart from Bitterness

O ne of the most dangerous spiritual toxins that can infiltrate the heart is bitterness. It is subtle at first—a hurtful word, a betrayal, or an unresolved wound—but if left unchecked, it festers into unforgiveness, resentment, and spiritual poison. Bitterness does not stay hidden; it seeps into every part of life, shaping how we think, feel, and even how we relate to God.

Hebrews 12:15 warns us, **"Looking diligently lest any man fail of the grace of God; lest any root of bitterness springing up trouble you, and thereby many be defiled;" (KJV).** Bitterness does not only harm the one who carries it—it contaminates others. True spiritual detox requires us to address unforgiveness and release forgiveness through the grace of God.

The Poison of Bitterness

Bitterness is like carrying a vial of poison and drinking it daily, hoping it harms the other person. Instead, it destroys the one who refuses to forgive. The spiritual, emotional, and even physical effects of unforgiveness are severe:

- **Spiritually** – It blocks prayers (**see Mark 11:25**), hardens the heart, and hinders intimacy with God.

- **Emotionally** – It fuels anger, depression, and cycles of negative thoughts.

- **Physically** – It contributes to stress, high blood pressure, and a weakened immune system.

Bitterness becomes a toxic chain that keeps people bound, unable to walk in freedom.

Forgiveness as Spiritual Detox

Forgiveness is not a feeling—it is a decision empowered by God's grace. It does not excuse wrongdoing, but it releases the toxic grip that offense has on the heart. Forgiveness cleanses the soul, making room for healing and peace.

Jesus taught us to pray, **"And forgive us our debts, as we forgive our debtors." (Matthew 6:12 - KJV).** Notice the connection—receiving forgiveness from God is tied to extending forgiveness to others. Detox requires letting go, because the heart cannot remain clean while holding onto grudges.

Biblical Examples of Forgiveness as Detox

1. **Joseph and His Brothers** – Though betrayed and sold into slavery, Joseph forgave, declaring, **"But as for you, ye thought evil against me; but God meant it unto good, to bring to pass, as it is this day, to save much people alive."**

(Genesis 50:20 - KJV). Forgiveness allowed him to see God's greater plan instead of being poisoned by revenge.

2. **Jesus on the Cross** – The greatest example of forgiveness came when Jesus said, **"Father, forgive them; for they know not what they do." (Luke 23:34 - KJV).** Even in agony, He released grace, teaching us that forgiveness is stronger than bitterness.

3. **Stephen the Martyr** – As stones crushed his body, Stephen prayed, **"Lord, lay not this sin to their charge." (Acts 7:60 - KJV).** His forgiveness broke the cycle of hatred and reflected the heart of Christ.

Why Forgiveness Is Hard but Necessary

Forgiveness detoxes, but it also costs something—it requires laying down our right to revenge. Many struggle with questions like:

- What if they don't deserve forgiveness?

- What if they never apologize?

- What if forgiving makes me weak?

The truth is: forgiveness is not about the offender, but about your freedom. Forgiveness is the key that unlocks your healing. It detoxes the soul by removing the toxic weight of offense and bitterness.

Forgiveness Brings Healing and Renewal

- **Forgiveness restores peace** – It clears the heart of turmoil and allows God's peace to reign.

- **Forgiveness opens the way for healing** – Emotional wounds begin to close when forgiveness is given.

- **Forgiveness restores relationships** – Not always through reconciliation, but through inner freedom that allows love to flow again.

- **Forgiveness realigns us with God's heart** – When we forgive, we mirror Christ and position ourselves for spiritual growth.

Practical Steps to Detox the Heart Through Forgiveness

1. **Acknowledge the Hurt** – Do not deny pain; confess it before God.

2. **Pray for the Offender** – Matthew 5:44 tells us to pray for those who hurt us; prayer softens the heart.

3. **Release the Right to Revenge** – Give justice into God's hands; He is the ultimate judge (**see Romans 12:19**).

4. **Speak Forgiveness Aloud** – Declare with your mouth, *"I forgive [name]. I release them into God's hands."*

5. **Repeat as Needed** – Sometimes forgiveness is a process; keep choosing it until the heart is free.

Reflection Questions

1. Is there anyone you still need to forgive to truly detox your heart?

2. How has bitterness shown up in your life—through anger, resentment, or distance from God?

3. Are you willing to release your pain into God's hands and choose freedom through forgiveness?

Prayer

Father, I come before You with the wounds in my heart. I confess the bitterness, resentment, and unforgiveness that I have carried. Today, I choose to forgive those who have hurt me, just as You have forgiven me through Christ. Wash me clean from every root of bitterness and fill me with Your love, peace, and healing. In Jesus' name. Amen.

Declaration

I declare that bitterness has no place in my heart. I release every offense, every wound, and every hurt into the hands of God. Through the power of forgiveness, I am detoxed, healed, and set free. My heart is filled with peace, and I walk in the liberty of Christ.

Chapter 17

The Role of Fasting – Detoxing Body and Spirit Together

Throughout scripture and church history, fasting has been one of the most powerful ways to detox both body and spirit. In a world overflowing with excess—food, entertainment, and distractions—fasting stands as a discipline of surrender. It quiets the body so the spirit can speak, and it humbles the soul before God.

Fasting is more than just skipping meals; it is a spiritual practice designed to cleanse, strengthen, and realign us with God. When done rightly, fasting brings a two-fold detox: it removes physical impurities from the body while simultaneously uprooting spiritual toxins such as pride, distraction, and unbelief.

Biblical Foundation of Fasting

The Bible is filled with examples of fasting as a way to draw closer to God and experience transformation:

- Moses fasted forty days on Mount Sinai as he received the Ten Commandments (**see Exodus 34:28**).

- Daniel fasted by refusing the king's food and choosing a simpler diet, leading to clarity, strength, and wisdom (**see Daniel 1:8–17**).

- Esther and her people fasted for three days before she risked her life to stand before the king (**see Esther 4:16**).

- Jesus fasted forty days in the wilderness, overcoming temptation and beginning His ministry in power (**see Matthew 4:1–2**).

These examples show us that fasting is not about starving the body, but strengthening the spirit and preparing the believer for God's work.

Fasting as a Natural Detox

From a natural perspective, fasting allows the body to rest, reset, and release toxins. Modern science has shown that fasting helps with:

- Cleansing the digestive system by giving it a break from constant processing.

- Balancing blood sugar and hormones, leading to clearer thinking and more energy.

- Boosting immunity, as the body focuses on repair instead of digestion.

- Breaking unhealthy food dependencies, helping us regain discipline over cravings.

118

Just as our bodies need physical cleansing, so too do our souls. Fasting brings harmony between the two.

Fasting as a Spiritual Detox

When practiced with prayer, fasting detoxes the soul by:

- **Breaking the power of the flesh** – Our cravings no longer dictate our obedience.

- **Sharpening spiritual sensitivity** – Fasting makes it easier to hear God's voice.

- **Humbling the heart before God** – Psalm 35:13 says, **"I humbled my soul with fasting." (KJV).**

- **Releasing spiritual strongholds** – Isaiah 58:6 declares, **"Is not this the fast that I have chosen? to loose the bands of wickedness, to undo the heavy burdens, and to let the oppressed go free, and that ye break every yoke?" (KJV).**

Through fasting, the clutter of life is stripped away, and the believer learns to depend solely on God.

Types of Fasts

Not all fasts look the same. Each has its purpose:

1. **Complete Fast** – Abstaining from all food for a set time, drinking only water.

2. **Partial Fast (Daniel Fast)** – Limiting diet to fruits, vegetables, and simple foods.

3. **Intermittent Fast** – Choosing certain hours of the day for fasting.

4. **Non-Food Fast** – Abstaining from television, social media, or other distractions to detox the mind and spirit.

The key is not the type of fast, but the heart behind it.

Fasting with the Right Heart

Jesus warned against fasting for show. In Matthew 6:16–18, He said, **"Moreover when ye fast, be not, as the hypocrites, of a sad countenance: for they disfigure their faces, that they may appear unto men to fast. Verily I say unto you, They have their reward. But thou, when thou fastest, anoint thine head, and wash thy face; That thou appear not unto men to fast, but unto thy Father which is in secret: and thy Father, which seeth in secret, shall reward thee openly." (KJV).**

True fasting is about intimacy with God, not public recognition. It should be accompanied by prayer, repentance, and time in the Word. Otherwise, it becomes a diet instead of a spiritual detox.

Results of Fasting

When fasting is done in alignment with God's will, the results are powerful:

- Renewed clarity and focus in hearing God's direction.

- Breakthrough in prayer, as spiritual resistance is broken.

- Healing and deliverance, as seen in Isaiah 58:8: **"Then shall your light break forth like the dawn, and your healing shall spring up speedily."**

- Spiritual empowerment, just as Jesus returned from His fast in the power of the Spirit (**see Luke 4:14**).

Fasting positions us to receive God's best by detoxing the body and purifying the soul.

Practical Guide for Fasting

1. **Set Your Intention** – Define why you are fasting: breakthrough, clarity, healing, or renewal.

2. **Prepare Physically** – Gradually reduce heavy foods before starting; drink water.

3. **Pair It with Prayer** – Fasting without prayer is only dieting.

4. **Fill the Space with the Word** – Replace meals with time in scripture and worship.

5. **End Gently** – Break the fast with light, healthy foods.

6. **Journal the Journey** – Record what God speaks to you.

Reflection Questions

1. How have you allowed your body's cravings or distractions to lead you more than the Spirit?

2. What type of fast is God calling you to embrace in this season?

3. Are you willing to surrender your physical comfort for deeper intimacy with Him?

Prayer

Lord, I humble myself before You in fasting and prayer. Cleanse my body, mind, and spirit from all impurities and distractions. Strengthen me to discipline my flesh so that my spirit may be fully aligned with Your will. As I fast, draw me closer to You, and let this be a season of clarity, healing, and breakthrough. In Jesus' name. Amen.

Declaration

I declare that fasting renews my body and refreshes my spirit. I am not bound by cravings or distractions; I am led by the Spirit of God. As I humble myself in fasting, I step into new levels of strength, clarity, and breakthrough. My body is detoxed, my spirit is empowered, and I walk in divine alignment with God's will.

Chapter 18

Guarding the Gates – Detoxing What You See, Hear, and Speak

Our spiritual lives are heavily influenced by what we allow through the gates of our soul. The eyes, ears, and mouth serve as entry and exit points that can either feed our spirit with life or contaminate it with toxins. Just as a physical detox requires us to watch what we consume, a spiritual detox demands that we carefully guard these gates.

Many believers fall into defeat, not because of outright rebellion but because of the slow, steady intake of polluted words, images, and sounds. Over time, these toxins affect our thoughts, weaken our faith, and hinder our intimacy with God. Detoxing what we see, hear, and speak is therefore not optional—it is essential for spiritual health.

The Eye Gate – Detoxing What You See

The eyes are powerful windows to the soul. What we look at can either build us up or break us down.

- Biblical Warning: **"I will set no wicked thing before my eyes" (Psalm 101:3 - KJV).**

- Jesus' Teaching: **"The light of the body is the eye: if therefore thine eye be single, thy whole body shall be full of light." (Matthew 6:22 - KJV).**

If our eyes are constantly filled with violence, lust, greed, and vanity, then our spirit becomes contaminated. Social media, television, and entertainment often flood us with images that normalize sin. To detox, we must practice discernment, discipline, and redirection:

- **Discernment** – Recognizing when an image or influence is harmful.

- **Discipline** – Turning away, even when the flesh craves it.

- **Redirection** – Choosing to fix our eyes on things above (**see Colossians 3:2**).

Guarding the eye gate means we refuse to look at things that stir temptation or weaken purity. Instead, we choose to gaze on the beauty of the Lord (**see Psalm 27:4**).

The Ear Gate – Detoxing What You Hear

What we hear shapes our faith. Faith comes by hearing the Word of God (**see Romans 10:17**), but fear, doubt, and compromise also come by hearing—toxic conversations, gossip, slander, and negative music corrupt the soul.

- Proverbs 18:8 warns: **"The words of a talebearer are as wounds, and they go down into the innermost parts of the belly." (KJV).**

- 2 Timothy 4:4 describes those who will **"turn away their ears from the truth, and shall be turned unto fables." (KJV).**

To detox the ear gate, we must:

1. **Filter Conversations** – Refuse to entertain gossip, lies, or negativity.

2. **Feed on God's Word** – Listen to sermons, worship, and scripture daily.

3. **Flee Corruption** – Remove music or content that glorifies sin.

The ear gate can either build faith or drain it. Detoxing means intentionally choosing sounds that align with heaven.

The Mouth Gate – Detoxing What You Speak

The mouth is both a gate of intake and release. Words we speak reveal the condition of our hearts (**see Luke 6:45**). Toxic speech—complaining, cursing, gossip, or doubt—pollutes not just ourselves but those around us.

- Proverbs 18:21 declares: **"Death and life are in the power of the tongue: and they that love it shall eat the fruit thereof." (KJV).**

- Ephesians 4:29 urges: **"Let no corrupt communication proceed out of your mouth, but that which is good to the** use of edifying, that it may minister grace unto the hearers." (KJV).

Detoxing the mouth gate means:

1. **Rejecting Negative Speech** – No longer agreeing with defeat, fear, or lies.

2. **Releasing Words of Faith** – Speaking the promises of God over every situation.

3. **Refreshing Others** – Using the tongue to edify and heal rather than tear down.

When the mouth is aligned with heaven, it becomes a fountain of blessing, not bitterness.

The Connection Between the Gates

The eyes, ears, and mouth are interconnected. What you watch influences what you think. What you hear influences what you believe. What you believe influences what you speak. And what you speak shapes your destiny.

Detoxing the gates is not about legalism, but about alignment. It's about making sure that nothing enters or leaves your life that poisons your walk with God.

Practical Ways to Guard Your Gates

- **For the Eyes:** Limit exposure to ungodly entertainment; fill your eyes with scripture and nature's beauty.

- **For the Ears:** Replace gossip with prayer, worldly music with worship, and lies with truth.

- **For the Mouth:** Practice declarations, gratitude, and blessing others daily.

- **Overall:** Ask the Holy Spirit to convict you when toxic influences try to enter.

Reflection Questions

1. What toxic things have you been allowing into your eyes, ears, or mouth without realizing their impact?

2. How can you realign your gates with God's Word and purity?

3. Are you willing to remove unhealthy influences, even if it costs you comfort or popularity?

Prayer

Father, I surrender my eyes, ears, and mouth to You. Cleanse every gate that has been polluted by the world, and guard me against toxic influences. Help me to fix my eyes on You, to open my ears to Your truth, and to speak words of life and blessing. Let my gates be consecrated to Your glory. In Jesus' name. Amen.

Declaration

I declare that my eyes are filled with light, my ears are tuned to truth, and my mouth speaks life. I reject every toxic influence and align my gates with the will of God. No poison shall enter or leave me; I am a vessel of purity, power, and purpose.

Chapter 19

Rest as a Detox – Releasing Stress and Finding God's Peace

In our fast-paced, constantly demanding world, rest is often seen as weakness. Society praises busyness, hustle, and endless productivity, while quietly neglecting the soul's desperate cry for renewal. Yet rest is not laziness—it is a spiritual discipline. It is one of the most powerful forms of detox that God designed for humanity.

When God created the heavens and the earth, He rested on the seventh day (**see Genesis 2:2–3**). Not because He was tired, but to establish a divine rhythm. Rest is more than sleep—it is an intentional pause that cleanses the body of stress, the mind of clutter, and the spirit of weariness. Without rest, toxins of anxiety, burnout, and emotional overload accumulate. With rest, God restores peace, clarity, and joy.

The Biblical Foundation of Rest

Rest is woven throughout scripture:

- **Sabbath Rest** – God commanded Israel to set aside one day each week to cease from work and focus on Him (**see Exodus 20:8–11**).

- **Jesus' Invitation** – **"Come unto me, all ye that labour and are heavy laden, and I will give you rest." (Matthew 11:28 - KJV).**

- **Spiritual Rest** – Hebrews 4:9 reminds us: **"There remaineth therefore a rest to the people of God." (KJV).**

Rest is not simply a break from work—it is communion with God. When we rest in Him, we detox from fear, stress, and striving, and we are filled with peace that surpasses understanding (**see Philippians 4:7**).

The Toxic Effects of Stress

Stress is one of the most subtle but deadly toxins in both the natural and spiritual life. It clutters the heart, weakens the immune system, and blinds us to God's presence. Many Christians carry stress like a badge of honor, thinking busyness equals effectiveness. But stress unaddressed leads to:

- **Physical burnout** – Fatigue, sleeplessness, illness.

- **Emotional heaviness** – Irritability, depression, and anxiety.

- **Spiritual distance** – Struggling to pray, worship, or hear God clearly.

Rest detoxes stress by forcing us to surrender control. It reminds us that God is the one sustaining our lives, not our frantic efforts.

Learning to Release Through Rest

True rest requires release. You cannot rest if you are still holding onto burdens.

- **Release Control** – Psalm 46:10 says: **"Be still, and know that I am God." (KJV).** Rest is letting go of the need to control outcomes and trusting God.

- **Release Stress** – Philippians 4:6–7 urges us to cast our anxieties on Him through prayer and thanksgiving.

- **Release Striving** – Striving comes from trying to earn God's approval. Rest detoxes the soul by reminding us that we are already accepted in Christ.

Rest is an act of faith. It declares: *"God, I trust You to handle what I cannot."*

Spiritual Rest vs. Physical Rest

Both dimensions are important:

- **Physical Rest** – Sleep, relaxation, and withdrawing from constant labor. This detoxes the body.

- **Spiritual Rest** – Worship, prayer, meditation on scripture, silence before God. This detoxes the soul.

One without the other leaves you incomplete. You can sleep eight hours, but still wake up anxious because your spirit has not rested.

Or you can spend hours in prayer, yet collapse physically because you've neglected the body. True rest integrates both.

Finding God's Peace Through Rest

Peace is not found in emptying your mind but in filling it with God's presence. Rest ushers us into peace when we:

1. **Pause Daily** – Create moments of silence where you simply sit in God's presence.

2. **Practice Sabbath** – Dedicate time weekly for worship and renewal.

3. **Pray and Release** – End each day by surrendering worries to God.

4. **Protect Boundaries** – Say no to constant demands that steal rest.

God's peace detoxes anxiety and replaces it with assurance. In rest, we remember that He is God and we are not.

Practical Detox Exercises

- **Detox the Body:** Take a full day without work or screens, giving your body permission to recharge.

- **Detox the Soul:** Journal your burdens, then pray and release them to God.

- **Detox the Spirit:** Meditate on God's promises of rest (**see Psalm 23, Matthew 11:28–30**).

- **Breath Prayer:** Inhale deeply while praying *"Lord, give me peace,"* and exhale slowly with *"I release my stress to You."*

Reflection Questions

1. Do you regularly honor God with times of rest, or have you allowed busyness to become an idol?

2. What toxins of stress, anxiety, or overwork do you need to release into God's hands?

3. How can you practice both physical and spiritual rest this week?

Prayer

Father, I come before You weary and burdened. I choose to lay down stress, striving, and worry at Your feet. Teach me to rest in You—not just in body, but in spirit and soul. Help me to guard the Sabbath of my life, to pause daily in Your presence, and to walk in Your peace. I receive Your rest as a gift today. In Jesus' name. Amen.

Declaration

I declare that I am no longer bound by stress or striving. I release every burden into God's hands and step into His rest. My body is renewed, my soul is restored, and my spirit is anchored in peace. I live in divine balance, free from the toxins of anxiety, fully refreshed in the presence of the Lord.

Chapter 20

Forgiveness as Detox – Letting Go of Emotional Poisons

Forgiveness is one of the most powerful forms of detox—yet it is also one of the hardest. Unforgiveness is like drinking poison and expecting the other person to die. It corrodes the soul, damages the body, and blocks the spirit from receiving God's flow of peace and blessing. Many Christians are saved but not free, because they are still carrying the toxins of bitterness, resentment, and anger deep in their hearts.

Forgiveness is not optional—it is essential. Jesus said in **Matthew 6:14–15, "For if ye forgive men their trespasses, your heavenly Father will also forgive you: But if ye forgive not men their trespasses, neither will your Father forgive your trespasses." (KJV).** To detox spiritually, emotionally, and relationally, forgiveness must become a lifestyle.

The Toxic Effects of Unforgiveness

Unforgiveness is a spiritual toxin that seeps into every part of life:

- **Physically** – Studies show bitterness raises blood pressure, weakens immunity, and causes chronic stress.

- **Emotionally** – Resentment fuels anxiety, depression, and emotional heaviness.

- **Spiritually** – Unforgiveness blocks prayer (**see Mark 11:25**), hinders worship, and keeps wounds open.

- **Relationally** – It poisons marriages, families, friendships, and even churches.

Like an untreated infection, unforgiveness spreads quietly until it controls every part of your being.

Forgiveness in the Bible

The Bible is filled with stories of forgiveness as detox and restoration:

- **Joseph** – Betrayed by his brothers, yet later declared, **"But as for you, ye thought evil against me; but God meant it unto good, to bring to pass, as it is this day, to save much people alive." (Genesis 50:20 - KJV).** He chose forgiveness, and it freed his destiny.

- **David and Saul** – David spared Saul's life multiple times, releasing vengeance into God's hands.

- **Jesus on the Cross** – The greatest example of forgiveness: **"Father, forgive them; for they know not what they do." (Luke 23:34 - KJV).**

Forgiveness is the key that unlocks freedom, while unforgiveness is the chain that binds the soul.

What Forgiveness Is—And Is Not

- **Forgiveness IS:** Releasing a person from the debt they owe you, surrendering the right to revenge, and allowing God to be Judge.

- **Forgiveness IS NOT:** Excusing the offense, denying the pain, or immediately restoring broken trust.

Forgiveness detoxes your heart, but reconciliation is a separate process. You can forgive, even if the other person never apologizes or changes.

The Spiritual Discipline of Letting Go

Forgiveness detox requires intentional release:

1. **Acknowledge the Pain** – Forgiveness is not pretending it didn't hurt. Healing starts with honesty.

2. **Surrender the Offense** – Place the offender and the offense at the foot of the cross.

3. **Pray for the Offender** – Jesus commanded us to pray for our enemies (**see Matthew 5:44**). Prayer detoxes bitterness.

4. **Repeat as Needed** – Sometimes forgiveness must be a daily choice until the wound is fully healed.

Forgiveness is both an act and a process. Each step removes another layer of poison until the heart is purified.

The Link Between Forgiveness and Freedom

Unforgiveness keeps you tied to the person who hurt you. It is like carrying them on your back everywhere you go. Forgiveness cuts the cord. It doesn't change the past, but it frees your future.

Jesus tied forgiveness to answered prayer: **"And when ye stand praying, forgive, if ye have ought against any: that your Father also which is in heaven may forgive you your trespasses." (Mark 11:25 - KJV).** In other words, your prayers detox and gain power when forgiveness flows.

Natural Detox Parallel

Just as the body cannot heal while toxins remain, the soul cannot heal while bitterness remains. Cleansing diets remove waste to allow nutrients to be absorbed. Likewise, forgiveness removes emotional poison, making space for love, peace, and joy to flow again.

Practical Forgiveness Detox Exercises

- **Write and Release:** Journal the names of those you need to forgive. Pray over the list, then tear it up as a prophetic act of release.

- **Cross Meditation:** Visualize placing the person and the pain at the foot of Jesus' cross. Leave them there.

- **Forgiveness Prayer:** Speak out loud: *"I forgive [name] for [offense]. I release them and bless them, in Jesus' name."*

- **Detox with Blessing:** Do one small act of kindness for someone who has wronged you (**see Romans 12:20–21**).

Reflection Questions

1. Who are you still holding in the prison of unforgiveness?

2. What has unforgiveness stolen from your peace, joy, or health?

3. Are you willing to release your offender to God and trust Him with justice?

Prayer

Lord Jesus, thank You for forgiving me when I did not deserve it. Today I choose to forgive those who have wounded me. I lay down bitterness, resentment, and anger, and I release every offense into Your hands. Heal my heart, cleanse my soul, and fill me with Your peace. Teach me to walk in forgiveness as a daily lifestyle. In Jesus' name. Amen.

Declaration

I declare that unforgiveness has no place in my life. I am free from bitterness, resentment, and anger. I release every offense into the hands of God. My heart is clean, my spirit is light, and my future is unbound. I walk in love, mercy, and freedom, fully detoxed by the power of forgiveness.

Chapter 21

The Word as Detox – Renewing the Mind Daily

Every day, our minds are bombarded with toxins—negative news, social media comparison, ungodly influences, self-doubt, and lies from the enemy. These pollutants, if left unchecked, contaminate our thoughts, shape our attitudes, and ultimately determine our actions. Romans 12:2 instructs us: **"And be not conformed to this world: but be ye transformed by the renewing of your mind, that ye may prove what is that good, and acceptable, and perfect, will of God." (KJV).**

The Word of God is the ultimate spiritual detoxifier. Just as water flushes toxins from the body, the Word flushes lies, fear, and confusion from the mind. When the Bible becomes our daily intake, it cleanses, strengthens, and renews us from the inside out.

Why the Mind Needs Detox

The human mind is like fertile soil: whatever seed is planted will grow. If the seeds are toxic—fear, anger, lust, doubt—then toxic fruit will appear in our lives. If the seeds are pure—faith, hope, love, truth—then spiritual fruit will abound.

Unrenewed minds are vulnerable to:

- **Negative Thought Cycles** – Rehearsing failure, rejection, or fear.

- **Worldly Influences** – Allowing media, culture, and peer pressure to dictate values.

- **Spiritual Blindness** – Believing lies that contradict God's truth.

A detoxed mind requires constant intake of God's Word to reprogram thought patterns and establish godly perspectives.

The Cleansing Power of the Word

The Bible often describes itself as water that washes and renews:

- **"Now ye are clean through the word which I have spoken unto you." (John 15:3 - KJV).**

- **"That he might sanctify and cleanse it with the washing of water by the word." (Ephesians 5:26 - KJV).**

God's Word detoxes the mind by:

1. **Exposing Lies** – It reveals when our thoughts don't align with God's truth.

2. **Replacing Darkness with Light** – It shifts our focus from fear to faith.

3. **Reprogramming Habits** – Daily reading builds new, godly neural pathways.

4. **Feeding the Spirit** – Just as food fuels the body, scripture fuels the spirit.

Jesus as the Living Word

John 1:1 declares, **"In the beginning was the Word, and the Word was with God, and the Word was God." (KJV)**. When we engage with scripture, we are engaging with Christ Himself. The Word is not mere text—it is a living, active power (**see Hebrews 4:12**).

Every scripture we read becomes spiritual nutrients. Every verse memorized becomes a weapon against the enemy. Every meditation cleanses the toxic build-up of the world.

Practical Daily Detox with the Word

1. **Morning Scripture Intake** – Begin each day with the Word before the world. Replace scrolling with scripture.

2. **Meditation Moments** – Pause throughout the day to meditate on one verse. Let it sink in.

3. **Speak the Word Aloud** – Confess promises to counter toxic thoughts. (for example: Replace "I can't" with **"I can do all things through Christ which strengtheneth me." – Philippians 4:13 - KJV**).

4. **Scripture Journaling** – Write verses and personal reflections, allowing the Spirit to reveal hidden toxins.

5. **Memorization** – Storing scripture in memory ensures a constant detox system (**see Psalm 119:11**).

Natural Detox Parallel

In natural detox, the body thrives on fresh, pure intake—clean water, whole foods, and nutrients that flush out toxins. Junk food and chemical-laden diets only add to the toxic overload. Likewise, the mind thrives on the fresh intake of scripture while toxic inputs— violent shows, gossip, negativity, worldly philosophies—must be reduced.

The Word is living water, hydrating the soul, nourishing the spirit, and flushing out mental pollution.

The Word as Weapon in Detox

When Jesus faced temptation in the wilderness, He countered every attack with, "It is written…" (**see Matthew 4:1–11**). The enemy's lies are spiritual toxins, but the antidote is scripture. Detox doesn't just cleanse; it equips. A Word-filled believer cannot be deceived because truth has saturated their thinking.

Reflection Questions

1. What voices or influences are shaping your thoughts more than the Word of God?

2. Do you treat daily scripture reading as a necessity for survival or as an option?

3. Which lies or toxic thoughts do you need to replace with God's promises today?

Prayer

Lord, wash my mind with the water of Your Word. Cleanse me from toxic thoughts, lies of the enemy, and worldly influences. Renew my thinking so that I may see life through the lens of Your truth. Plant Your Word deep within me and let it bear fruit in every area of my life. In Jesus' name. Amen.

Declaration

I declare that my mind is daily renewed by the Word of God. No toxic thought will take root in me. I live by truth, I walk in light, and I resist the lies of the enemy. The Word of God is my filter, my foundation, and my freedom.

Chapter 22

Worship as Detox – Clearing the Atmosphere of the Soul

When toxins build up in a physical space, the air feels heavy, suffocating, and unclean. In the same way, the soul can carry a spiritual heaviness—worry, stress, bitterness, and negativity—that clogs the atmosphere of our inner life. Worship is God's divine air purifier. It shifts the focus from ourselves and our problems to the greatness of God.

Psalm 22:3 declares: **"But thou art holy, O thou that inhabitest the praises of Israel." (KJV).** Whenever we worship, we create a sacred atmosphere where God's presence dwells, and where toxins lose their power.

Worship is not just about singing songs—it is a heart posture of surrender, reverence, and adoration that detoxes the soul and renews the spirit.

The Toxic Atmosphere of the Soul

Toxins in the soul often manifest as:

- **Heaviness** – carrying burdens without release (**see Isaiah 61:3**).

- **Fear and Anxiety** – consuming energy with "what ifs."
- **Bitterness and Resentment** – recycling pain from the past.
- **Negativity** – constant complaining or hopeless thinking.

These pollutants linger in the spiritual atmosphere like stagnant air. Worship sweeps them away, allowing God's glory to refresh and oxygenate the soul.

Worship as a Spiritual Purifier

1. **Shifts the Focus** – Worship moves attention from toxic thoughts to God's power.

2. **Releases the Burden** – When we exalt God, we simultaneously lay down the weight we were never meant to carry.

3. **Restores Joy** – True worship brings a spiritual lightness, replacing heaviness with gladness (**see Isaiah 61:3**).

4. **Invites God's Presence** – The enemy cannot thrive where God is exalted. Worship is a repellent to darkness.

The Atmosphere of Worship in Scripture

- **Paul and Silas in Prison (see Acts 16:25–26):** They worshiped in chains, and their praises not only broke their bonds but shifted the entire atmosphere, shaking the foundations of the prison. Worship not only detoxed their souls but also changed their surroundings.

- **Jehoshaphat's Battle (see 2 Chronicles 20:21–22):** As Judah went into battle, singers were appointed to praise God. Their worship became a weapon that confused the enemy.

- **David's Harp for Saul (see 1 Samuel 16:23):** David's worship drove away the tormenting spirit from Saul, proving that worship cleanses atmospheres polluted by oppression.

Natural Detox Parallel

In natural health, detoxing the air is essential. We open windows, breathe fresh oxygen, and use purifiers to clear toxins. Without fresh air, the body suffers fatigue, headaches, and weakness. Similarly, the soul requires fresh oxygen of worship to function at full capacity. When worship fills the atmosphere, toxins of despair, anger, and fear dissipate.

Worship as a Lifestyle, Not an Event

Worship is more than Sunday service—it is a daily practice. We worship when we:

- Choose gratitude over complaining.
- Lift our hands in surrender during trials.
- Acknowledge God in small victories.
- Offer our bodies as living sacrifices (**see Romans 12:1**).

When worship becomes a lifestyle, detox becomes ongoing. The air of the soul remains fresh, pure, and filled with the fragrance of God's presence.

Practical Ways to Detox with Worship

1. **Morning Praise Ritual** – Begin each day by speaking or singing praises before speaking to anyone else.

2. **Worship in Storms** – Sing, even when it hurts. Worship shifts the spiritual climate of trials.

3. **Instrumental Atmosphere** – Fill your home with worship music that changes the spiritual air.

4. **Spontaneous Worship** – Don't wait for a service; lift a song or prayer of adoration wherever you are.

5. **Sacrificial Worship** – Praise God, not for what He's done, but for who He is.

Reflection Questions

1. What toxins in your soul have been weighing down your spiritual atmosphere?

2. How often do you practice worship outside of church gatherings?

3. Do you invite God's presence through worship daily, or only when you are in crisis?

Prayer

Father, I lift my heart, voice, and life to You in worship. Cleanse my soul of heaviness, bitterness, and fear. Let my worship rise as a sweet fragrance before You, purifying my atmosphere. Teach me to worship, not just in church, but in every moment of my life. May my soul be continually refreshed in Your presence. In Jesus' name. Amen.

Declaration

I declare that worship clears the atmosphere of my soul. The heaviness is lifted, fear is broken, and joy fills my spirit. My worship invites God's presence and repels every toxin of darkness. I live as a worshipper, and my atmosphere is purified daily by His glory.

Chapter 23

Prayer as Detox – Flushing Out the Soul's Burdens

P rayer is more than a ritual or religious duty—it is a divine exchange. When we pray, we empty our hearts of worry, fear, and sin, and receive God's peace, strength, and wisdom in return. Just as natural detox flushes harmful substances out of the body, prayer flushes out the toxins of the soul.

Philippians 4:6–7 reminds us: **"Be careful for nothing; but in every thing by prayer and supplication with thanksgiving let your requests be made known unto God. And the peace of God, which passeth all understanding, shall keep your hearts and minds through Christ Jesus." (KJV).**

Through prayer, burdens are lifted, peace flows in, and the soul is cleansed of the toxic buildup that comes from life's battles.

The Toxins Prayer Removes

Prayer is God's detox pipeline. It draws out:

- **Worry and Anxiety** – The mental clutter that robs peace.

- **Fear and Doubt** – The toxins that paralyze faith.

- **Unconfessed Sin** – The guilt and shame that poison the soul.

- **Unforgiveness** – The bitterness that stagnates spiritual growth.

- **Weariness** – The heaviness of carrying life's pressures alone.

When these toxins are released through prayer, the soul regains its strength, clarity, and purity.

The Detox Power of Prayer in Scripture

1. **Hannah's Cry (see 1 Samuel 1:10–18)** – She poured out her soul before the Lord and left with peace, even before her situation changed. Prayer detoxed her despair.

2. **David's Psalms (see Psalm 51:10)** – He confessed, **"Create in me a clean heart, O God."** David's prayers were spiritual cleansing baths.

3. **Jesus in Gethsemane (see Luke 22:41–44)** – In deep anguish, Jesus prayed until His burden was released and He was strengthened to face the cross. Prayer flushed out His sorrow and filled Him with resolve.

Natural Detox Parallel

In natural health, detoxification often involves flushing toxins out through hydration and elimination. The body requires water to carry waste away. Without it, toxins accumulate, causing fatigue, headaches, and disease. Similarly, prayer is the living water (**see**

John 7:38) that flushes spiritual waste. Without prayer, toxins of sin, stress, and fear accumulate, leaving the soul sluggish and weighed down.

Prayer as a Daily Detox Discipline

Prayer should not be reserved for crises—it must become a daily detox habit. When we pray consistently, we prevent toxic buildup in the soul. Jesus modeled this lifestyle: **"And in the morning, rising up a great while before day, he went out, and departed into a solitary place, and there prayed." (Mark 1:35 - KJV).**

Like daily cleansing, prayer keeps the inner life fresh and pure.

Practical Ways to Detox Through Prayer

1. **Confession Cleansing** – Begin prayer by repenting and asking God to wash away sin (**see 1 John 1:9**).

2. **Burden Exchange** – Verbally release your worries to God, replacing them with His promises.

3. **Gratitude Shift** – Start listing blessings to push out negativity.

4. **Scripture-Soaked Prayers** – Pray God's Word to renew the mind and flush out lies.

5. **Silent Detox** – Sit quietly in God's presence, letting His Spirit purify anxious thoughts.

Reflection Questions

1. What burdens or worries do you need to release to God in prayer today?

2. Do you view prayer as a duty or as a cleansing lifeline for your soul?

3. Are you practicing daily prayer as a preventative detox, or only when in crisis?

Prayer

Lord, I come to You to release the burdens of my soul. Wash away my fear, worry, sin, and weariness. Cleanse me with Your presence and refresh me with Your Spirit. Teach me to pray daily as a spiritual detox that keeps me pure, strong, and renewed. In Jesus' name. Amen.

Declaration

I declare that prayer is my spiritual detox. I will not carry worry, fear, or guilt—I release them through prayer. My heart is cleansed, my mind is renewed, and my spirit is refreshed. I walk in peace, strength, and purity because I daily commune with God.

Chapter 24

Fasting as Detox – Cleansing Both Body and Spirit

F asting is one of the most powerful tools God has given us for both spiritual renewal and physical cleansing. In the natural, fasting allows the body to reset, remove toxins, and heal from the constant demands of food digestion. In the spiritual, fasting empties the soul of distractions and sharpens our focus on God.

Jesus Himself declared in Matthew 6:16–18 that fasting was not a suggestion but an expectation: **"When you fast..."**—not if. He modeled this discipline when He fasted forty days in the wilderness (**see Matthew 4:2**), gaining strength to resist temptation and launch His ministry.

Fasting is both a detox of the body and a detox of the soul, aligning us with God's power, purity, and purpose.

The Dual Detox Power of Fasting

Physical Detox

- Allows the body to rest from digestion.
- Promotes cellular repair and healing.

- Flushes out toxins accumulated from unhealthy foods.
- Boosts energy, clarity, and longevity.

Spiritual Detox

- Breaks the grip of fleshly desires and addictions.
- Sharpens spiritual sensitivity and discernment.
- Cleanses the soul of pride, distraction, and sin.
- Opens the heart to deeper intimacy with God.

When combined, fasting brings harmony to spirit, soul, and body—leading to transformation that neither diet nor prayer alone can produce.

Biblical Examples of Fasting as Detox

- **Moses (see Exodus 34:28)** – Fasted 40 days on Mount Sinai and returned radiant with God's glory.

- **Esther and the Jews (see Esther 4:16)** – Fasted for deliverance, resulting in national salvation.

- **Daniel (see Daniel 10:3)** – Practiced a partial fast, refusing rich foods to seek God's revelation.

- **The Early Church (see Acts 13:2–3)** – Fasted for direction, leading to the launch of missionary journeys.

Each example shows fasting as a reset button—detoxing from the ordinary to embrace the extraordinary.

Natural Detox Parallel

When we fast, the body goes into a healing mode called autophagy, where damaged cells and toxins are broken down and recycled. Spiritually, fasting creates a similar effect. God clears away old mindsets, toxic habits, and spiritual clutter to bring renewal. Just as the body repairs itself during fasting, the spirit becomes sharpened, purified, and empowered.

The Misconceptions About Fasting

Many view fasting as starvation or punishment, but it is not about deprivation—it's about substitution. We set aside physical food so we can feast on the Word of God (**see Matthew 4:4**). True fasting is not simply skipping meals; it is replacing food with prayer, worship, and scripture meditation. Without that substitution, fasting is merely a diet.

Practical Ways to Fast for Detox

1. **Water Fast** – Abstaining from all food, drinking only water (for short durations).

2. **Daniel Fast** – Eating fruits, vegetables, nuts, and water for a set period.

3. **Partial Fast** – Skipping one or two meals a day and dedicating that time to prayer.

4. **Media or Soul Fast** – Removing non-food toxins such as social media, TV, or gossip.

Choose the type of fast God leads you to, focusing on both body cleansing and spiritual renewal.

The Right Heart in Fasting

Isaiah 58 warns that fasting is meaningless if done without the right spirit. True fasting involves humility, compassion, and obedience to God. When we fast with the right heart, it becomes a powerful detox for pride, selfishness, and spiritual stagnation.

Reflection Questions

1. What physical or spiritual toxins is God calling you to release through fasting?

2. Do you approach fasting as a duty or as a life-giving detox?

3. How can you incorporate fasting into your lifestyle, not just as an occasional event, but as a rhythm of spiritual renewal?

Prayer

Lord, as I fast, cleanse both my body and my spirit. Remove every toxin that weighs me down, and make me sensitive to Your voice. Replace my hunger for earthly things with a hunger for righteousness. May my fasting bring healing, freedom, and breakthrough. In Jesus' name. Amen.

Declaration

I declare that fasting is my divine detox. My body is renewed, my soul is cleansed, and my spirit is sharpened. I will walk in discipline, strength, and clarity. As I fast, God is breaking chains, releasing power, and positioning me for victory.

Chapter 25

Guarding the Gateways – Protecting the Mind, Heart, and Spirit

E very believer has spiritual gateways—entry points through which influences, ideas, and spirits can enter the soul. These gateways include the eyes, ears, mouth, heart, and mind. Just as a house has doors and windows that must be secured, your life has spiritual openings that must be guarded.

Proverbs 4:23 reminds us: **"Keep thy heart with all diligence; for out of it are the issues of life." (KJV).**

If the heart is the wellspring of life, then guarding the gateways is not optional—it is a divine mandate. Unprotected gates allow toxic influences to enter, while guarded gates keep the spirit pure, clean, and strong.

The Eyes: The Window of the Soul

Jesus said in Matthew 6:22–23: **"The light of the body is the eye: if therefore thine eye be single, thy whole body shall be full of light. But if thine eye be evil, thy whole body shall be full of darkness. If therefore the light that is in thee be darkness, how great is that darkness!" (KJV).**

- What you watch matters. Whether movies, social media, or environments, what enters through your eyes deposits into your spirit.

- Visual temptations are real. Lust, jealousy, comparison, and discontent often begin with the eyes.

- Practical Guardrails:

  - Be intentional about what you consume visually.

  - Replace toxic media with uplifting, faith-filled content.

  - Train your eyes to seek God's glory in creation and people.

The Ears: The Gate of Influence

Romans 10:17 says: **"So then faith cometh by hearing, and hearing by the word of God." (KJV).** Just as faith is built by hearing God's Word, fear, doubt, and sin can be birthed by listening to toxic words.

- **Conversations carry power.** Gossip, negativity, and curses contaminate the spirit.

- **Music has spiritual influence.** What you listen to either builds faith or feeds flesh.

- Practical Guardrails:

- Surround yourself with life-giving voices.
- Limit exposure to negative conversations.

- Fill your ear gate with scripture, sermons, and worship.

The Mouth: The Gate of Expression

Proverbs 18:21: **"Death and life are in the power of the tongue." (KJV).**

The mouth is both an entry gate (what you eat and confess into your soul) and an exit gate (what you release into the atmosphere).

- **Words shape your spirit.** Negative confessions attract bondage, while faith-filled words release freedom.

- **Diet affects your spirit.** Natural food choices influence clarity, energy, and discipline, which impact your spiritual life.

- Practical Guardrails:

    - Speak blessings, not curses.
    - Avoid idle talk, gossip, and complaints.
    - Practice speaking the Word daily.

The Heart: The Core of Belief and Emotion

The heart is the control center of your life. It is where love, bitterness, hope, and fear reside. If the heart is contaminated, the entire life reflects that contamination.

- **Bitterness is poison.** Unforgiveness clogs the heart's flow.

- **Idolatry invades the heart.** Anything we love more than God becomes toxic.

- Practical Guardrails:

  - Practice forgiveness as a daily discipline.

  - Keep your heart tender through prayer and worship.

  - Allow God's Word to continually cleanse hidden motives.

The Mind: The Battlefield of the Spirit

The mind processes what the eyes see, the ears hear, and the heart feels. Romans 12:2 instructs: **"And be not conformed to this world: but be ye transformed by the renewing of your mind, that ye may prove what is that good, and acceptable, and perfect, will of God." (KJV).**

- **Toxic thoughts weaken the spirit.** Fear, lust, pride, and worry can pollute your soul.

- **Godly meditation strengthens discernment.** What you meditate on, you magnify.

- Practical Guardrails:

  - Capture negative thoughts and replace them with scripture (**see 2 Corinthians 10:5**).

- Train your mind to focus on what is pure, noble, and praiseworthy (**see Philippians 4:8**).

- Avoid overexposure to media that feeds fear or confusion.

Natural Detox Parallel

Just as detoxing the body requires controlling what enters through the mouth (food), skin (environment), and lungs (air), so does spiritual detox require guarding the entry points of the soul. A body that is constantly exposed to toxins cannot stay clean, and a spirit exposed to ungodly influences cannot remain pure.

The Benefits of Guarding the Gateways

- **Spiritual clarity** – You discern God's voice more easily.

- **Emotional stability** – Toxic thoughts and feelings lose power.

- **Purity of heart** – A guarded heart produces holiness.

- **Protection from deception** – Guarded gates block the enemy's schemes.

- **Overflowing life** – Clean gates allow God's Spirit to flow freely through you.

Reflection Questions

1. Which gateway—eyes, ears, mouth, heart, or mind—do you need to guard more intentionally?

2. What small changes can you make this week to reduce toxic inputs?

3. How can you replace negative influences with life-giving ones?

Prayer

Father, I thank You for giving me the ability to guard my gates. Help me to be vigilant with what I see, hear, say, and allow into my heart and mind. Purify every doorway of my soul and make me a temple filled with Your Spirit. In Jesus' name. Amen.

Declaration

I declare that my eyes see light, my ears hear truth, my mouth speaks life, my heart remains pure, and my mind is renewed daily by the Word of God. I am protected by the blood of Jesus, and no toxic influence can enter my spirit. My gates are guarded, and I walk in holiness and strength.

Chapter 26

A Lifestyle of Purity and Holiness

Spiritual detox is not a one-time event; it is the beginning of a lifestyle of purity and holiness. Many believers experience breakthroughs in prayer, fasting, or revival services, but without daily commitment, they soon drift back into old habits and polluted environments. To live detoxed, we must pursue holiness as a way of life, not just an occasional practice.

Holiness is not perfectionism—it is alignment with God's will. Purity is not isolation—it is consecration to God's purpose. Together, purity and holiness create a shield that protects us from spiritual toxins and keeps us effective as vessels of honor for God's kingdom (**see 2 Timothy 2:21**).

What Purity Means in a Contaminated World

We live in a society where impurity is normalized. Entertainment glorifies immorality, business celebrates greed, and even within the church, compromise is often tolerated. In such an environment, pursuing purity can feel like swimming against a strong current.

Purity, however, is not just about abstaining from sin; it is about singleness of devotion. It is the state of being undivided in heart toward God (Psalm 24:3–4). A pure life is one where our thoughts, motives, words, and actions are filtered through God's holiness.

The Call to Holiness

Scripture is clear: **"Be holy, for I am holy" (1 Peter 1:16).** Holiness is not optional—it is God's expectation for His children. Holiness means to be set apart—different from the world, reflecting God's nature in every sphere of life.

Living holy does not mean living in legalism or trying to earn God's approval. Rather, holiness is a fruit of intimacy with God. The more time we spend in His presence, the more we reflect His purity.

Habits That Sustain Purity

1. Guarding the Mind.

2. Fill your thoughts with God's Word (**see Philippians 4:8**).

3. Refuse to entertain toxic images, conversations, or influences.

Sanctifying the Body

- Treat your body as God's temple (**see 1 Corinthians 6:19–20**).
- Eat, rest, and live in ways that honor Him.

Purifying Speech

- Speak life, not gossip or negativity (**see Ephesians 4:29**).
- Words should be seasoned with grace, reflecting Christ.

Renewing Relationships

- Choose friendships that sharpen your faith (**see Proverbs 27:17**).
- Let go of toxic connections that corrupt good morals (**see 1 Corinthians 15:33**).

Living Transparently

- Walk in honesty, humility, and integrity.
- Darkness loses power where there is light.

Natural Detox Parallel

Just as maintaining a natural detox requires ongoing discipline—choosing whole foods, staying hydrated, exercising, and avoiding toxins—maintaining spiritual detox requires continual choices toward purity. Skipping one healthy meal does not destroy your body, but constant indulgence in junk food leads to sickness. Likewise, one misstep in the Christian walk does not disqualify us, but a pattern of neglect will erode holiness.

Rewards of a Pure and Holy Lifestyle

1. **Closeness to God** – Purity clears the channel for prayer and intimacy.

2. **Spiritual Authority** – Holiness gives weight to our words and prayers.

3. **Peace of Mind** – Purity eliminates guilt and shame.

4. **Powerful Witness** – A holy life is a silent sermon to the watching world.

5. **Preparedness for Heaven** – Without holiness, no one will see the Lord (**see Hebrews 12:14**).

Practical Steps to Remain Detoxed

- **Practice daily repentance** – keep short accounts with God.

- **Maintain accountability** – walk with mentors and peers who challenge your growth.

- **Engage in regular fasting and prayer** – sharpening your spiritual senses.

- **Stay Word-centered** – using scripture as the filter for every decision.

- **Cultivate worship as a lifestyle** – not just an event but a daily offering.

Reflection Questions

1. What areas of your life still need the cleansing fire of God's holiness?

2. Have you allowed subtle toxins to creep back in—through thoughts, habits, or relationships?

3. What daily practices can you implement to protect your spiritual purity?

Prayer

Lord, I desire to live a life that pleases You in every way. Cleanse me from hidden faults and make me sensitive to Your Spirit. Please give me the strength to walk in purity when the world offers compromise. Set me apart for Your purpose, and let holiness be my testimony. In Jesus' name. Amen.

Declaration

I declare that I am set apart for God's glory. My heart is pure, my mind is renewed, and my body is a temple of the Holy Spirit. I will not be conformed to the world but transformed by the renewing of my mind. I walk in holiness, not by my strength, but by the Spirit of God within me. My life is a living sacrifice, holy and acceptable unto God.

Conclusion

The Final Charge: A Life Detoxed and Fully Alive

A Journey Completed, A Lifestyle Begun

You have walked through the journey of Spiritual Detox—from identifying the toxins that pollute the soul, to embracing the cleansing power of God, to learning the disciplines of prayer, fasting, worship, forgiveness, and renewal. But remember, this is not the end—it is the beginning of a lifestyle.

Just as natural detox restores health and vitality to the body, spiritual detox restores clarity, strength, and holiness to the spirit. God does not desire His children to live in cycles of toxicity, compromise, or bondage. He has called you to freedom, wholeness, and fullness of life.

The Call to Vigilance

Your greatest danger after this journey is to slip back into old patterns. The enemy waits for opportunities to reintroduce toxins into your spirit. That is why the charge of Jesus is so critical: **"Watch and pray, that ye enter not into temptation" (Matthew 26:41 - KJV).**

- Be vigilant against spiritual laziness.

- Be mindful of what you allow into your eyes, ears, and heart.

- Be intentional about feeding your spirit with God's Word daily.

Detox is not about restriction—it is about freedom. It is about clearing away the clutter so the presence of God can flow unhindered.

A Call to Holiness and Power

The church and the world need believers who are spiritually detoxed—pure vessels that God can use for His glory. Paul reminds us in 2 Timothy 2:21: **"If a man therefore purge himself from these, he shall be a vessel unto honour, sanctified, and meet for the master's use, and prepared unto every good work." (KJV).**

When you remain cleansed and consecrated:

- You walk in boldness, not fear.

- You live in peace, not anxiety.

- You carry fire, not ashes.

- You become a witness of the kingdom, shining as light in darkness.

The Final Detox Parallel

Think of the body: when it is free of toxins, energy increases, focus sharpens, and life feels renewed. Spiritually, the same is true. Detox brings:

- **Clarity of mind** – you hear God clearly.
- **Purity of heart** – your motives align with His will.
- **Strength of spirit** – you resist sin and stand firm.
- **Joy of the Lord** – you overflow with peace and power.

This is not temporary; this is the abundant life Jesus promised (**see John 10:10**).

A Charge to You

I charge you, beloved reader, to:

- Guard your heart with diligence (**see Proverbs 4:23**).
- Walk daily in renewal (**see 2 Corinthians 4:16**).
- Keep the fire burning (**see Leviticus 6:13**).
- Pursue holiness without compromise (**see Hebrews 12:14**).
- Be a vessel of revival in your family, church, and community.

Do not let this book be another read that gathers dust. Let it become your daily practice, your lifestyle, your testimony.

Reflection Questions

1. What toxins are you most prone to allow back into your life, and how will you guard against them?

2. How will you hold yourself accountable to remain spiritually detoxed?

3. What daily practices from this book will you carry forward as part of your permanent walk with God?

Final Prayer

Father, I thank You for the journey of spiritual detox. Cleanse me continually, Lord. Guard me from the snares of the enemy and strengthen me to live in holiness. Let my life be a temple where Your Spirit dwells freely. May I remain pure, steadfast, and overflowing with Your power. In Jesus' name. Amen.

Final Declaration

I am free.

I am cleansed.

I am renewed.

I am a vessel of honor, set apart for God's glory.

No toxin of sin, fear, bitterness, or distraction has power over me.

I live a detoxed life—spirit, soul, and body—fully surrendered to Christ.

From this day forward, I walk in freedom, purity, and power.

www.ingramcontent.com/pod-product-compliance
Lightning Source LLC
LaVergne TN
LVHW021448080426
835509LV00018B/2213